W9-AQT-725

THOMAS PRINGLE

by John Robert Doyle, Jr.

In Thomas Pringle South Africa inherited from Scotland, among the 1820 Settlers, an already established poet and editor, then entering his thirties and anxious to edit (or do any work appropriate to his training and talents) for a living and to write poems for posterity. In the first hope he failed completely and after six years left South Africa forever. Despite the brevity of his residence, the time proved sufficient, and he bequeathed to this new land a small body of verse which was to become the foundation of a national literature. For the first century of the country's life verse makers came and went, but almost none achieved anything that approached permanence. Pringle alone continued to be the one poet pointed to with confidence.

Only with the advent of the twentieth century, and indeed well into the century, did South Africa produce a writer in verse who could claim literary significance. After this point was passed, Pringle began to recede into history and assume his place as the *founder* rather than "the lone poet." The judgment of time has been just. Thomas Pringle left writing which emerged from the South African environment. Since what he wrote was of the country, it can truly belong to that land.

Yet in addition to the poems, which appeared in *African Sketches* (1834) a few months before his death at forty-five, is the second half of the volume, which he called *Narrative of a Residence in South Africa*. Deriving from the journal he kept from the moment of his arrival in Simon's Bay, the *Narrative of a Residence* has been very widely accepted as one of the finest pieces of prose and most valuable descriptive and historical documents to come out of South Africa during the early nineteenth century. It was immediately popular upon publication and today is a joy to the reader, a century and a half after its composition was begun in 1820.

TWAYNE'S WORLD AUTHORS SERIES (TWAS)

The purpose of TWAS is to survey the major writers —novelists, dramatists, historians, poets, philosophers, and critics—of the nations of the world. Among the national literatures covered are those of Australia, Canada, China, Eastern Europe, France, Germany, Greece, India, Italy, Japan, Latin America, the Netherlands, New Zealand, Poland, Russia, Scandinavia, Spain, and the African nations, as well as Hebrew, Yiddish, and Latin Classical literatures. This survey is complemented by Twayne's United States Authors Series and English Authors Series.

The intent of each volume in these series is to present a critical-analytical study of the works of the writer; to include biographical and historical material that may be necessary for understanding, appreciation, and critical appraisal of the writer; and to present all material in clear, concise English—but not to vitiate the scholarly content of the work by doing so.

Thomas Pringle

By JOHN ROBERT DOYLE, JR.
The Citadel

Twayne Publishers, Inc. :: New York

Library of Congress Catalog Card Number: 73-187635

MANUFACTURED IN THE UNITED STATES OF AMERICA

In memory of my father
Who would have understood Thomas Pringle

Preface

F. York, Pho.

THOMAS PRINGLE

analyze fully what he accomplished there. To this study I have summoned whatever resources I may have in an effort to understand one additional unit in the literature of South Africa—and thus ultimately of the Western world.

During the period of composition I have been aided by a grant from The Citadel Development Foundation, which relieved me of certain teaching duties. To the foundation and to Major General James W. Duckett, president of The Citadel, I express my deep appreciation for this assistance. Also I am deeply grateful to Professor A. C. Partridge, who located for me a copy of *Glen-Lynden: A Tale of Teviotdale* and who furnished the information used in the bibliography to describe this very rare volume.

J. R. D., Jr.

The Citadel
Charleston, South Carolina

Acknowledgments

The author offers grateful acknowledgment to the following for permission to quote from various books.

C. Struik, (Pty.) Ltd., Thomas Pringle's *Narrative of a Residence in South Africa,* with introduction, biographical, and historical notes by A. M. Lewin Robinson, Cape Town, 1966.

Maskew Miller, Ltd., *None Daring To Make Us Afraid,* A Study of the English Periodical Literature of the Cape Colony from Its Beginnings in 1824 to 1835, by A. M. Lewin Robinson, Cape Town, 1962.

A. A. Balkema, *Thomas Pringle, His Life and Times,* by Jane Meiring, Cape Town and Amsterdam, 1968.

Eric, Mark, and John Pringle, *Pringles of the Valleys,* Adelaide, Cape Province, 1957.

Eric Pringle, *These Are My People,* Adelaide, Cape Province, 1967.

The Bodley Head, *The Collected Poems of Roy Campbell,* London, 1955.

Routledge & Kegan Paul, Ltd., *The Koisan Peoples of South Africa,* London, 1951.

Library of Parliament, South Africa, Fairbairn Letters (Unpublished).

I wish to thank in a very special way Dr. A. M. Lewin Robinson, of the South African Library, Cape Town, for the assurance I have drawn from his books, articles, and personal letters. To him and his staff at the South African Library, I offer appreciation for a copy of the portrait of Thomas Pringle and for photocopies of the Fairbairn Letters as well as of rare materials in early magazines.

Contents

Chronology

1789 Born January 5, on a farm called Blaiklaw, four miles from Kelso, in Roxburghshire.

1794 Attended school with his two older brothers, William and John.

1795 Death of his mother. His father married again later.

1802 Sent to Kelso Grammar School.

1805 In November entered Edinburgh University

1808 During February became a clerk in the General Register Office.

1811 Published, with Robert Story, "The Institute," a satire on the Edinburgh Philomanthic Society.

1816 Contributed several poems to *Albyn's Anthology* and published "Autumnal Excursion" in *The Poetic Mirror.*

1817 Became a joint editor of *The Edinburgh Monthly Magazine* (Blackwood's) and also about the same time of *The Star.* Married Margaret Brown on July 19. In October became a joint editor of Constable's *Edinburgh Magazine.*

1819 Published his first volume of poems, *The Autumnal Excursion and Other Poems.* Composition of "The Emigrant's Farewell."

1820 Sailed from Gravesend for South Africa, February 15, in the brig *Brilliant.* Reached Simon's Bay, April 30, after a voyage of seventy-five days. Sailed from Simon's Bay on May 10 and reached Algoa Bay on May 15. Disembarked May 25 and started inland on June 13. Reached Roodewal, on the Great Fish River, June 21, and arrived on the Pringle location June 29.

1821 Made first extended trip into parts of South Africa seldom visited, starting March 25. In June the acting governor, Sir Rufane Donkin, visited the Eastern Province, and Pringle was granted an interview. A few weeks after his interview with Sir Rufane, he went with Robert Hart on an excursion into the Albany district. On one of his exploring trips, he climbed the Winterberg, 7,778 feet.

1822 Trip in April with officers and saw his first elephants. In July William Pringle, the eldest brother, arrived with his family and other relatives from Scotland and took possession of the farm at Eildon, Baviaans River. Thomas prepared to proceed to Cape Town to accept a position to which he had been appointed in the new South African Library. After a short stay at Somerset Farm, Thomas and his wife and her sister left Graaff-Reinet for Cape Town, August 17. The party reached Cape Town September 25.

1823 February 3, Pringle and the Reverend Abraham Faure sent a memorial to the governor requesting permission to start a magazine. John Fairbairn arrived October 10. He and Pringle opened their Classical and Commercial Academy on December 1. On December 2, Pringle was told that he could start a magazine, which was to become the *South African Journal*.

1824 First number of the *South African Commercial Advertiser* appeared January 7 and the second January 14. With the third number, Pringle and Fairbairn entered the editorial and literary division of the paper. First issue of the *South African Journal* was published March 5 and the second May 7. What Pringle called the Cape "Reign of Terror" against freedom of the press started May 7. Set out on an excursion through the interior, October 8, with W. T. Blair and Captain W. Miller, East India Company. An accident which fractured his thigh bone ended the trip and required an extended period of mending. Returned to Cape Town early in December. Published in London *Some Account of the Present State of the English Settlers in Albany, South Africa*.

1825 Left Cape Town for Algoa Bay on February 11. Visited Port Elizabeth, Uitenhage, Enon, Kowie River, Graham's Town (March 20), and moved through the Albany area. July 1, met by appointment Dr. John Philip, author of *Researches in South Africa* and superintendent of L.M.S. stations, at Somerset, and proceeded to Graaff-Reinet for a visit with Captain Sir Andries Stockenstrom. On December 19 bade farewell to Pringle family at Glen-Lynden and started toward Port Elizabeth.

1826 Embarked for England on April 16 (probable date) and arrived in London July 7. Article in the *New Monthly Magazine* for October seemingly led to his appointment as secretary of the Anti-Slavery Society.

1827 Took up his duties as secretary of the Anti-Slavery Society in March.

1828 Published in London *Ephemerides: or Occasional Poems, Written in Scotland and South Africa* and *Glen-Lynden: A Tale of Teviotdale.*

1833 On August 28, Parliament passed the bill which abolished slavery.

1834 Thomas had finished his *Narrative of a Residence in South Africa.* This was published along with his South African poems under the title *African Sketches,* and in May he sent a copy to John Fairbairn in Cape Town. On June 27 a document presenting the Act of Abolition, signed by Thomas Pringle, was published. Slavery was formally abolished August 1. June 27 was also the date of the beginning of the illness which took Thomas Pringle's life on December 5. He was buried in the cemetery at Bunhill Fields, London.

CHAPTER 1

Scotland Was First

UNPREDICTABLE, and strange indeed are the forces that guide man's destiny, forces over which even modern man with his vast knowledge has no control and with all of his sophistication little understanding. Rational explanations are helpless before events. Why, for example, should the son of a Scottish farmer, lamed by an accident in infancy and moving through life on crutches, sent to the university rather than the field—why should this delicate and handicapped son of Scotland—be the man called upon to lead his father's family into the wild areas of the Cape Province, to engage in a bitter struggle for freedom of the press in Cape Town, to leave the country in seeming personal defeat and financial ruin—and then become with justice known as the father of South African poetry in English?

Capable of complete obliviousness to what should have been obvious, Thomas Pringle was passionately intent upon certain ends but doubted other accomplishments which since his death the world has considered valuable. He died knowing some of the work he had done was leaving a mark upon mankind, but it may be questioned that he believed his poems would survive. Actually, for more than half a century what he had written of the country and its people dominated South African verse.

Even less sure than his hope that he would achieve some measure of poetic immortality is the evidence that he grasped the value of his prose, especially some parts of it. Acutely observant, energetic, meticulous in his attention to details, Pringle became a valuable recorder of the Cape environment of both native and European life in the South Africa of the 1820's. The account which he wrote of his years there seems to have been considered by Thomas himself as something of an introduction to, even explanation of, his South African poems. Most of these poems he looked upon as records rather than proper poetic creations. In this appraisal he was essentially correct, yet there was about his writing something which gave South Africa the start it needed.

Within himself Pringle encompassed a sea of contending tides. During his fifth year in South Africa, in 1825, he wrote one of his closest friends, "I have always cherished at the bottom of my heart the ambition of writing some day or other a little volume of poetry worthy of being preserved. A very small portion of what I have yet written is in my own sincere opinion of that description. But some 'fair future day' I still hope to write something that may not dishonour Scotland." [1] Yet simultaneously he confessed, "At present however I almost feel criminal in giving up any portion of my heart or time to poetry. I am sensible of the vast importance of the task I have undertaken—& I will not flinch from it. . . . I am not yet fairly warmed to the work, & I fly to versifying like a man with an evil conscience who flies to drink to drown tomorrow." [2] The situation which had motivated this letter was Pringle's presence on the frontier, after opposition by the governor had made his remaining in Cape Town essentially impossible. Without employment and in debt, he returned to his family at Glen-Lynden. Here with the conditions of the native peoples constantly before him, he began to turn toward the feeling that their relief was the goal which he had in life, rather than the fighting for freedom of the press at the Cape, which had brought him into violent conflict with the governor, Lord Charles Somerset. Accordingly, he began to move in a nonliterary direction and to disdain the making of verses as worthy of his time. His letter, however, reveals that he would never be able to discard his love of poetry and his hope that his lines would insure for him some kind of reputation here on earth.

Years later, back in England and with his employment as secretary of the Anti-Slavery Society almost completed, he concerned himself once more, in a very specific way, with the hope of being remembered for his poetry. In this letter he is asking for a biography after his death, and he offers to begin furnishing the materials to the person being requested to write it. It is in this letter that he again evaluates himself as a poet.

> . . . no one knows better than I do the real value of my poetical vein. But though I have (as yet at least) written but a few pages that deserve to live in the literature of my country; yet I may without pre-

sumption, perhaps, rank myself among those "Minors" who have indited, whether from genius or good luck, a few things which their countrymen "would not willingly let die." If I am not presumptuous, therefore, in hoping that my poetic trifles may survive for a little while . . . I may be excused for the vanity of anticipating that a brief memoir . . . may be required from some friendly pen, to accompany my "Remains." [3]

When Pringle referred to "my country," he was thinking of Scotland. It was South Africa, however, which was to give his family its fortune and him a reputation. Had Thomas lived out his life in Scotland, he probably would have been quickly and easily forgotten. Though his stay in the Cape was brief, during the time that he was there South Africa needed Thomas Pringle, and he in turn required the situation and raw materials which this new land could offer.

I *How It All Began*

Certainly it would be very difficult to have a more complete attachment to the soil of a country than the family of Thomas Pringle had to Scotland. Coming from Selkirkshire, the family can be traced "back to the ancient house of Whytbank." [4] These Pringles of Whytbank lie buried in Melrose Abbey. In the thirteenth century the name had been Hoppryngil, Robert de Hoppryngil being the first name recorded. The fourteenth century spelling had become Hoppringill. During the sixteenth century, it was shortened to Pringill, and by the end of the seventeenth century had assumed its present form. Thomas himself seemed aware of the history of his family for at least four generations and remarked that his people had lived on the land during that time. The land upon which Thomas was born had been leased by his father Robert and grandfather William. Named Blaiklaw, also called "Easterstead," the farm of nearly five hundred acres was about four miles south from Kelso, in the parish of Linton, Roxburghshire. The author's mother was the daughter of Thomas Haitlie, a farmer in Berwickshire, and his wife Margaret the daughter of William Brown, an East Lothian farmer.

There are two reasons for stressing the farming heritage of Thomas Pringle. One is that it appears in complete contrast to his own editorial and literary life. Another is that the farming background became not only useful but perhaps decisively important during the early South African years.

Death came to Thomas Pringle December 5, 1834, exactly a month before his forty-sixth birthday. Thirty of these years were spent in Scotland, ten in England, and six in South Africa. Of the period in South Africa, two years and four and a half months covered the entire time of residence in Cape Town and the remainder was with his family on their newly acquired land or in exploratory travel throughout the Cape. Only the London era took him far away from family and farm, but even in London his work often fastened his attention upon the rural areas of South Africa, where his immediate family lived.

Acute farmers and canny Scots that they were, the Pringles made the correct choice each time a decision was forced upon them. As a result, the family of Robert Pringle succeeded from the very first in the bold transplanting venture that took them thousands of miles from their homeland and introduced them to the undeveloped regions of the Eastern Cape. As a result of shrewd and informed decisions, hard work, adaptability, and intelligent foresight, the Pringles became one of the important building families of South Africa. After giving all proper credit to Robert Pringle and his sons William and John, the historian should not forget Thomas in this whole undertaking, for it was he who held the place as official head of the party of Scots, twenty-four in number, which sailed on the *Brilliant* for South Africa early in 1820. Furthermore, students of the situation are inclined to the opinion that the idea of emigration to the Cape originated with Thomas. That Thomas made the practical arrangements for the move is simple fact.

Though it would be inaccurate to suggest that the Pringles' decision to leave Scotland was inevitable, events of the preceding quarter of a century made this move a thoroughly predictable one. Thomas Pringle, the third of seven children, was born January 5, 1789. Thus, this child started life on the eve of the French Revolution, an event whose ideological aspects were for many years to cast their influence across Europe and Britain. In his thinking and his actions, Thomas was caught in the pervasive tide of these ideas. It also seems to be quite true that his temperament from even his earliest years was sympathetic in part to the kind of thinking the movement of his era was promoting.

In opposition to these concepts, however, powerful environmental facts and events need to be considered.

Perhaps it is no exaggeration to claim that the direction of Pringle's whole story was decided by what is alleged to have been an accident, an event which occurred when he was three months old. According to the frequently told account, he was dropped by his nurse, Nanny Potts, and his leg was dislocated at the hip. All versions of this action say that Nanny, terrified at what had happened, revealed nothing. When the baby was finally taken to a doctor in Kelso, the physician found it too late to correct the damage. Nevertheless, when Thomas was three and still unable to walk, another determined effort was made to correct the injury—without success. At this point, the child assumed the crutches upon which he was to move through life.

Whether Thomas Pringle was dropped by his nurse or mother or someone else, whether his dislocated leg stemmed from another source, is not ultimately important. His lameness was a fact, and the first result was the effect that his physical plight had upon his developing temperament. Early accounts (based upon Pringle's own written statement concerning the events of his childhood) [5] report that in her attempts to compensate for what had happened, Nanny Potts lavished her attentions upon the child to the point of either creating or developing serious character deficiencies. Thomas became headstrong and unmanageable. Finally, his parents had to intervene and demand stricter discipline. The whole situation was of sufficient gravity for Pringle later in life to remark upon his behavior. The importance of all of this is found in the suggestion that the man never quite recovered, or believed he had not recovered, from the damage which was done to the child. Thus, these early events should be recalled when one comes to examine aspects of his life such as his relationship to the governor of the Cape during the struggle for freedom of the press in South Africa.

More immediate and obvious was the effect that the lameness had in restricting the actions of a growing boy. For Thomas, outdoor games were impossible, and he would have to desert the farming tradition of his family. Early aptitudes must have suggested to his parents the possibility of an academic career, for after elementary training he was at thirteen sent to Kelso Grammar School, which had been attended by Sir Walter Scott. Three years later, in November, 1805, his father decided that he should go on to Edinburgh University, where he would be able to prepare for one of the professions.

Though Thomas did enter the university and though there was never any question of his academic ability, it was quickly evident that he was not directing his efforts toward preparing for any of the professions, nor was he interested in a degree—but that attitude was quite usual at the time. What quickly manifested itself was an absorbing attachment to literature, at the time not a part of a university course. His knowledge of English poetry was above that of those with whom he associated, and his concern passed beyond the realm of the reader into that of the writer. From these early years at the university to the end of his life, few days passed in which something was not written—letters, entries in his journal, essays, poems. From the beginning Thomas Pringle fulfilled the first quality for becoming a writer: he wrote—he did not merely talk about it.

Though above all else Thomas wished to make his living as a writer, the first requirement when he left the university was any employment which would allow him to live. Accordingly, he accepted a place in the General Register Office. Though the salary was small, it offered a certain income, and here the young man remained for a number of years, 1808 to 1817. He wrote, certainly, but there was as yet little income from his efforts. His first poem had been published in 1811, but it was not until 1816 that "Autumnal Excursion" created some significant reaction and at least one extremely practical effect. The poem was read and admired by Sir Walter Scott, and this established a relationship which Pringle used as long as Scott lived, until 1832. None of this writing, however, was of much immediate economic assistance.

Suddenly, in 1817, the whole situation changed. During April, Pringle accepted a place as joint editor of *The Edinburgh Monthly Magazine,* a new publication being started by young William Blackwood. This undertaking was subsequently to become famous as *Blackwood's Edinburgh Magazine,* under the editorship of John Gibson Lockhart and John Wilson. The magazine was founded as a Tory journal to oppose the powerful Whig *Edinburgh Review.* The irony of this whole affair is that though Thomas Pringle had the literary ability which Blackwood recognized, his thinking and politics were distinctly in the Whig direction. Even if he had been a Tory, Thomas Pringle's ability, training, and temperament did not qualify him for either attack or defense in the political turmoil which seethed around him. Added to all else, John Cleghorn, his co-editor, was completely inadequate. The outcome was inevitable. Blackwood was justifiably disappointed with the first number. When he attempted to make suggestions, he discovered that now—as when a child and later at the Cape—Thomas Pringle refused in even the least way to be what he called "led or fettered by any person." [6] Thus, while the third number was in the press, the owner gave his editors three months' notice. In the midst of the conflict, Blackwood discovered that Cleghorn and Pringle had arranged to assume the editorship of Constable's *Scot's Magazine* as soon as their contract with him expired. Meanwhile, Pringle was also editor of the Edinburgh *Star*, described by Josiah Conder, Pringle's first biographer, as "almost the only liberal paper in Scotland." [7]

In July, 1817, Pringle married Margaret Brown, who was nine years older than he. Loss of his letters and journals must have destroyed information about Margaret and his published writing says almost nothing about her. As a result, little is known about his wife except the obvious economic situation which she created at a crucial period. At the time of their marriage, Thomas does not seem to have been able to bring her to Edinburgh to live with him. His economic problem was not an individual one. His family was not only unable to assist him; they, too, needed help. His father had been forced to leave Blaiklaw in possession of his son William and was working in England on a farm hired at Auckland. A decline in agriculture, however, reached far beyond the Pringles; in fact, there was general economic stress throughout Scotland and England. Britain, along with Europe, was struggling through the effects attendant upon the Napoleonic wars. For some months [8] after he left Blackwood, Thomas had attempted to live by adding to his income from freelance writing. This was clearly impossible, and he returned to the Registry Office, where the income was certain, regardless of how small.

At this time a letter to a friend makes very definite his state of mind:

It is sufficient to say that my present occupation is inadequate to the support of my family in the most moderate way I can devise; I see little or no prospect of materially improving my circumstances in this country; and I have already incumbrances on my shoulders which threaten every day to become heavier, and at last to overwhelm me in hopeless debt. Now this is a state of life the most intolerable that can well be imagined, and which one must experience fully to estimate. It paralyses the very blood and heart of man; and I cannot and will not endure it, while a prospect remains of extricating myself by any exertion, or sacrifice, that can be made with honour and a good conscience.[9]

Looking back, Pringle could see only that which suggested a lack of success. Various opportunities as an editor had brought him nothing. Though some of his poetry had received favorable notice, writing of verse would never contribute much to his income. Had he been twenty he might have had more hope, but he had already used up the years of his twenties. His letter makes clear that he understood a decision was being made in desperate circumstances. Soon it was obvious that the choice was not whether to remain in Edinburgh, Scotland, the British Isles, or even Europe. Thomas now began to consider whether there was any place in the world where he might hope to succeed.

II *The Great Decision*

Evidence of precisely what ideas passed through Pringle's mind, and especially the order of occurrence, is at this removal in time impossible to assemble. The sequence of the family's actions, however, makes the general situation clear. His brother Alexander had already gone to America and his father to England. The remaining brothers were considering the possible areas of the world to which they might move, and the sisters of the family seemed destined for domestic service. Thousands in Britain and Europe were trying to solve the same problem. That the condition was general and serious is attested by the action taken in Parliament. The government appropriated money, not without unannounced reasons, to send out some several thousand settlers to the Eastern Cape. Passage fees were reasonable; grants of free land were to be made available; and supplies and implements were to be offered at cost. The demand for places seems to have been immediate and great. Estimates suggest that between fifteen and twenty applicants asked for each available passage. Finally between four and five thousand were selected, and the great move started.

Whether it was Thomas or another member of the Pringle family who suggested leaving Scotland may never be known and is perhaps not very important. What is significant, however, is the immediate action and sustained leadership displayed by Thomas following the government's announcement of its plans for the settlement at the Cape. After family conferences, Thomas made the application to the Colonial Department and thus in both name and fact became head of the group, which was to become known as the Scottish party. With energy and ability Thomas Pringle began to plan for his whole family to leave Scotland and England. He now turned to great advantage his literary acquaintance with Sir Walter Scott, who upon request used his influence with important government officials. The Pringles were not only accepted as settlers but were given free passage to South Africa. Since Thomas was not physically able to become a farmer, he sought some type of civil employment. Scott was able to secure letters from influential people in London to the governor of the Cape. Something of the arrangements involved may be noted in a letter Pringle wrote Scott, from Deptford, February 5, thinking their ship was to sail on the next day: "I have got letters from Mr. Barrow and others to the Colonial Secretary & to other individuals of influence. Mr. Barrow also told me that he & Mr. Croker had got Mr. Goulburn to promise a letter of introduction for me to the Governor from the Colonial Office. It has not yet been sent in to me but may perhaps to-morrow before we sail. When you arrive in London and forward the packet you so kindly promised it may be addressed to the care of Mr. Ellis the Colonial Secretary, with whom I shall leave directions respecting it." [10] Obviously, here is evidence of how hard Thomas was pressing his relation with Scott for his family and to his own advantage. Subsequently he was appointed to a place in the South African Public Library, Cape Town, at the beginning of its existence.

Evidently, Scott had made a sincere effort to help because he wrote Pringle that he believed his young friend would be "put on as good if not a better footing than any who go out to the Cape." [11] The free passage to South Africa was perhaps the first evidence of Scott's help; next, the letters Thomas carried with him must have created considerable effect upon those to whom Pringle introduced himself when the ship reached Cape Town and later Algoa Bay. The appointment to the library was the last indication that Scott's support was effective.

After various delays, the Pringle party of twenty-four persons sailed from Gravesend on February 15, 1820. They were aboard the *Brilliant*, a 331-ton brig, along with a party of 120, from Surrey, and enough additional passengers to make a total of "a hundred and fifty-seven souls,"[12] as Thomas records it. The *Brilliant* sailed into Simon's Bay, Cape of Good Hope, on April 30, following an uneventful voyage of seventy-five days. Land was welcome, but it was a strange scene which greeted these Scottish and English eyes.

CHAPTER 2

Learning a New Country

EVENING shadows drifted across Simon's Bay toward the sterile sands and bleak hills beyond as the *Brilliant* dropped its sails and moved toward the South African shore. It was April 30, early winter, and as the new arrival slipped through the water she found at anchor several other emigrant ships, some of which had sailed from England a month earlier than her own time of departure. Not enough light remained by which to see the new land, but with morning everyone was on deck. The first reaction was recorded in a Scots brogue: "Hegh, sirs! but this is an ill-favoured and outlandish-looking country. I wad fain hope, that thae hieland hills and muirs are no fair sample o' our African location?" [1] Actually the scene before them was not like the lands upon which they were to settle. Thomas Pringle explained to the speaker that their grants would be very different from the soil upon which he gazed. Different indeed the country to which they were going would be, but Thomas was perhaps wrong in what he imagined. He, too, was moving toward visual images and a life which a year before nothing within him could have conceived. Now, however, their unseen home had to remain in abeyance, for business details required his time during the ten days before the ship sailed on to its destination.

Because Thomas was official head of the Scottish party, he was allowed to land and go into Cape Town. Here he met Colonel Bird, colonial secretary, and discussed with him details concerning the settlement of the Pringle party in the Eastern Cape. From Colonel Bird he learned that not only was the governor in England but the letter which Thomas brought could not be opened by another person because it was marked private. While in the city, he did, however, meet various important persons and discovered a maternal cousin who proved helpful in supplying information and provisions. After a profitable period on shore, he returned to the *Brilliant,* which sailed on May 10 for the last part of its journey.

I *The New Country*

Beginning at dawn on May 1, 1820, Thomas Pringle became a gatherer of information about this country in which he was now seeking so much—and where he found even more than he knew. There was, he understood, much to be learned, and he approached his new home with his journal on his knee and a pen in his hand. Concerning Cape Town he wrote that it was too well known to need any word from him; but once he had rounded the Cape, observation and comment seemed relevant. Here is the first scene, viewed from the ship's deck, to be recorded in his *Narrative of a Residence in South Africa:*

> . . . On the 12th, at day-break . . . we found ourselves almost becalmed, nearly opposite the entrance to the Knysna, a fine lagoon, or salt water lake, which forms a beautiful and spacious haven (though unfortunately rather of difficult access) winding up . . . into the very bosom of the magnificent forests which cover this part of the coast . . . we kept tacking off and on within a few miles of the shore. This gave us an excellent opportunity of surveying the coast scenery of Auteniqualand and Zitzikamma, which is of a very striking character. The land rises abruptly from the shore in massive mountain ridges, clothed with forests of large timber, and swelling in the back ground into lofty serrated peaks of naked rock. As we passed headland after headland, the sylvan recesses of the bays and mountains opened successively to our gaze. . . .[2]

Starting with lakes, forests, mountains–whatever loomed before him—Thomas Pringle displayed something of an obsession for gathering information about everything he encountered. Upon the entrance of the *Brilliant* into Algoa Bay, he was soon ashore, noting topography, plants, piles of implements, groups of settlers —whatever was in sight. Having exhausted the supply of items along the shore, he borrowed a pony and started inland to Bethelsdorp, located some nine miles from the coast. A Hottentot boy was his guide and trotted at the side of his pony. Arriving at the mission at sunset, Thomas remained for the night, and returned to his ship the next day. At Bethelsdorp he for the first time was brought into contact with the Caffer (modern Kaffir) peoples and heard the language of the Amakosa tribe.

Perhaps the most important day in the history of the Pringle family was June 6, 1820. The acting governor, Sir Rufane Donkin, arrived at Algoa Bay and conferred with Thomas concerning the location of the settlers from Scotland. The government had decided to offer the Pringles a mountainous tract of land more than a hundred miles from the coast. The specific area marked for the Pringles was the upper part of the valley formed by the Baviaans River. The grant was adjacent to the Kaffir frontier. It was planned to settle the territory to the east with five hundred Highlanders and a smaller group from the west of Scotland. Sir Rufane explained to Thomas that he could exercise his option of asking for land nearer the coast, among the English settlers. After conferring with members of his party, Thomas officially accepted the highland valley. The other Scots never arrived, but the Pringles had made a wise decision. In their isolated location, they prospered, while the settlers nearer the coast often encountered insurmountable difficulties.

II *Moving Inland*

After various delays, the settlers aboard the *Brilliant* disembarked, and Thomas was busy with all of the arrangements connected with securing needed supplies and transportation into the interior. Everything, of course, was done with the official assistance of the government. Finally, on June 13, the family of Robert Pringle and their associates—a total of twelve men, six women, and six children—started for their location, estimated to be a hundred and seventy miles by the route which it was necessary to travel. There were seven wagons, each drawn by from ten to twelve oxen, owned and directed by Dutch residents of the area. Natives, especially Hottentots, were employed in manning the wagons.

Once on the way, Thomas Pringle's first display of leadership was to persuade (with the help of a gift of tobacco) the drivers to detour by a salt lake where his party would be able to secure a supply for the coming year. This action demonstrated that Thomas had already been gathering information, for he had learned of this salt pan from his reading. Also, he had prepared himself by studying the language of the Dutch "boors," as he called them, with whom he was now dealing. The designation "boor," present "Boer," is merely the word for farmer, and the language which Thomas was finding so useful was what is now *Afrikaans*.

As twilight gathered, the group outspanned and established a camp for the night. Here Thomas observed and for the first time recorded the habits of the various peoples with whom he was coming in very close contact. He remarked upon the gigantic size of many of the Boers, observed the eating and drinking of each group, noted preparations for the night, listened to the various languages being spoken, speculated upon what might be beyond the circle of light created by the camp fire. As rapidly as possible, he was absorbing all around him that was new—though not appearing to consider how much this world might absorb him. One thing is certain: the environment through which he was traveling was not static.

Laboriously the wagons moved inland at slightly less than fifteen miles a day. Half a dozen rivers were crossed, most of them dry or almost dry, and Thomas showed awareness of the vast differences in the various areas through which they passed. Arriving June 21 at Roodewal, now Cookhouse, a military post on the Great Fish River, the party received an excellent example of South African hospitality. Many others were to follow. In addition to the joys of social association with men and women from England and Scotland, Thomas here met the first of several men to whom he was to turn often for information and expert advice—which he followed immediately and completely. Not all but certainly much of the success of Robert Pringle's family in South Africa started with the competent direction which Thomas sought and used.

Before leaving Roodewal, the Pringle party was furnished with new wagons, drivers, and attendants. At the end of the first day's journey, they were joined by an armed escort, designated by the government to accompany them to their location. To many of the 1820 Settlers, the information that they were entering dangerous territory must have come as a profound shock. Little did they suspect before sailing from England that they were being used to create an area of defense against native tribes to the east. Before he left this country, however, Thomas Pringle was to learn about the conflicts existing among the peoples of southern Africa.

Meanwhile, his little group pushed on into an area where wagons could be pulled only with great effort. At one point, no more than three miles were covered in two days—a wagon at times having thirty oxen pulling it.

III *Possession*

Finally, the emigrants moved through the last poort, or pass, and standing on elevated ground looked out upon the land which they were to possess. According to the frequently repeated story, the Dutch-African field cornet turned to the party with, "And now, mynheer, *daar leg uwe veld*—there lies your country." Speaking for the settlers from Scotland, Thomas wrote:

> . . . Looking in the direction where he pointed, we beheld, extending to the northward, a beautiful vale, about six or seven miles in length, and varying from one to two in breadth. It appeared like a verdant basin, or *cul de sac,* surrounded on all sides by an amphitheatre of steep and sterile mountains, rising in the back-ground into sharp cuneiform ridges of very considerable elevation; their summits being at this season covered with snow, and estimated to be from 4,000 to 5,000 feet above the level of the sea. The lower declivities were sprinkled over, though somewhat scantily, with grass and bushes. But the bottom of the valley, through which the infant river meandered, presented a warm, pleasant, and secluded aspect; spreading itself into verdant meadows, sheltered and embellished, without being encumbered, with groves of mimosa trees, among which we observed in the distance herds of wild animals–antelopes and quaggas–pasturing in undisturbed quietude.[3]

Speaking at the moment of looking out upon the valley, one man in the party is reported to have said, "Sae that's the lot o' our inheritance, then? Aweel, now that we've really got till't, I maun say the place looks no sae mickle amiss, and may suit our purpose no that ill, provided thae haughs turn out to be gude deep land for the pleugh, and we can but contrive to find a decent road out o' this queer hieland glen into the lowlands—like ony other Christian country." [4]

Exactly six months had elapsed between the day the Pringles had left Scotland and the day they looked out over the area which was to be a new home. Temporary arrangements were made for the first night, and the next morning a party started out to explore the valley. The day following, July 1, Captain Harding, a deputy landdrost of Cradock, arrived with a surveyor and formally installed the Pringles on their lands. Before leaving, Captain Harding advised Thomas to guard against surprise attacks from Bushmen or Kaffirs. The captain considered the Pringle position an exposed one. Following his advice, men of the group began immediately to stand night watch, despite the fact that there were only twelve available, including Robert Pringle, now sixty-seven.

Having set their guard against surprise attack from native tribes, the little body was stunned when introduced to the first of the great wild animals, a lion at midnight. Thomas reports that when he was wakened from sleep, he at first assumed a storm had broken upon them. Understanding his mistake, he reached for his gun and hurried out into the night—there to be joined by the other men, who had acted in the same manner. In debate they attempted to determine the direction from which the roar had come, but no decision was reached. Uncertain and fearful, they fired their guns in all directions, built the camp fire to a great blaze, and finally threw torches into the darkness. With little doubt the lion had retreated. Several days later, while cutting reeds in the river bed, the occupied workers were startled when a large lion rose from the reeds nearby. He jumped to the bank, paused to gaze at them, then slowly withdrew. During the winter and spring, on several occasions lions visited the new settlement, though without injury to anyone or the domestic animals. Later appearances were more serious, and very soon Thomas used "the lion" as his subject in both prose and verse.[5]

Exploration, protection, and temporary cover had been required first. Housing came next, since it was winter. Into all of this work Thomas entered, despite his crutch. The buildings were erected in the local manner, showing how rapidly the Pringles were absorbing South African ways. The ingredient of final importance, however, was that these settlers from Scotland brought with them their own traditions, concepts, and skills by which they tested the South African life around them. The value of the resultant depended upon the balance which could be maintained between the old and the new—what had been imported from the civilization of Europe and what was found in Africa.

Immediately obvious to Thomas was the need which they had

for animals. Dogs were used for protection and hunting; horses were required for movement about the country but also for hunting. The value of sheep and cows they understood from past experience. Large numbers of oxen were employed for plowing and wagon duty. Except horses, none of these animals was hard to find or expensive. Very soon a representative from each family of the settlement went out on a purchasing expedition. When spring approached, the Pringle party was equipped to turn its attention to clearing land, running irrigation ditches, and beginning to plow. Along with other planting, the planting of orchards was not neglected.

How busy Thomas was in settling his family in their adopted country may be seen by examining entries in his journal for these early days. One week, July 6, after their arrival he sent two men to Roodewal, from which they had just come, to place an order for supplies, and he addressed a letter to a Lieutenant Stretch asking him to buy a horse or two for the Pringles. On July 12 a soldier arrived with one horse, in answer to this request. The same day Thomas hired a Boer named Engelbrecht to assist with his wagon in transporting tents, goods, and building materials from one part of their location to another. Letters arrived on July 17 assuring Thomas that soon ten armed Hottentots would be placed under his command for protection, thus relieving the new arrivals of guard duty. The Hottentots reported on July 25. Meanwhile, July 18 Thomas and his brother John, with Black William, undertook a more extensive exploration of the valley than had been attempted the first day. Perhaps the primary information they wished was to learn what lay immediately beyond their valley. Because of the need to do many things quickly, Thomas had on July 13 rejected an invitation from Mr. Hart to go with him into Kaffirland. Invitations of this type, however, Thomas was soon to accept.

Concerning all of this activity, only a small part of which has been indicated, Thomas wrote, "I thus found myself all at once, and not a little to my own surprise, performing the novel and somewhat incongruous functions of a sort of civil and military officer, or a medical practitioner, religious instructor, engineer, architect, gardener, plasterer, cabinet-maker, and, I might add, *tinker*. In short I was driven to do the best I could in the peculiar position in which circumstances had placed me; and when (as was frequently the case) my own knowledge and the experience of others failed me, I was obliged to trust to 'mother-wit.' "[6]

Clearly, "mother-wit," or at least the mental element in the equation, again and again was to demonstrate its value. The Pringles' grasp of their situation is demonstrated by the analysis they made of the prospects inherent in the location to which they had been assigned. According to the original plan of the government, the Pringles received a hundred acres for each man in the group, a total of eleven hundred acres. Before they left Scotland the area seemed adequate, but they were quick to understand that on the Baviaans River location traditional farming would be unprofitable. At this distance from the coast, crops could be grown only by using irrigation; but not enough water existed in the locality to irrigate more than 50 to 60 percent of the land. The Pringles also saw that even had they been able to grow for sale a crop such as wheat it would not have returned a profit after figuring the cost of transportation to the coast. The one possible source of income to be gained from the land as it now existed was the raising of sheep and cattle, and they would need far more land for this purpose. Thus, Thomas made a request to the government for an enlargement of their grant. The reply offered more acres at the present location or removal to a new location. Before giving an answer for the Pringles, Thomas sought information from Mr. Hart, at Somerset Farm. Upon his advice, the party from Scotland accepted the extension of their present location. Before they had plowed the first yard of soil or planted a seed, the family of Robert Pringle was thinking of the years ahead.

IV *Journeys*

Starting with his visit to Somerset Farm during the second half of September, 1820, Thomas Pringle made a number of journeys through various areas of the Cape. Regardless of the primary purpose of the trip, seldom did he go anywhere without turning his movements into an information-gathering expedition. In this first instance, seeking advice before making a specific decision was his reason, but he used the occasion to visit with a Dutch farmer and record in detail what he saw. Beginning with the dogs that rushed out to challenge his arrival, Thomas missed little that crossed his vision. Remembering what his family was in the process of doing, he noted the architectural methods used in building, the clothing of the family, food and drink being served, gardening and orchard arrangements, land under cultivation, the specific number of sheep and cattle, the use of irrigation, and the method and speed of grinding grain. Actually, he must have found the answer to his question here—before he reached Mr. Hart and proposed the query to him. What he was learning was, first, how to survive in Africa and, second, how to employ certain natural elements to human advantage.

Having heard that his Dutch hostess was an expert in the making of leather clothing, Thomas ordered a traveling jacket of dressed springbok skin and trousers of the same skin, to be faced with leopard fur. The following day he bade farewell to his host and hostess, and after a pleasant and profitable visit with Captain Harding the next night Thomas continued his journey and spent the following night with a man who specialized in breeding horses—his area being well suited to what he had decided to raise. Then Thomas went on to Somerset Farm and saw for the first time a large area of land under cultivation. Here, on the government's experimental area, Mr. Hart had through skill and persistence converted swamp soil into farmland. For the new arrival, the entire trip offered a valuable lesson in adaptation. Each person he visited had used his locality to produce the things for which it was best suited. Even without advice, he now knew that the Pringles would be wise to fit themselves to the requirements of the land they had been granted.

Though he had declined the first invitation, nine months after his arrival at Baviaans River, which the Scots renamed Glen-Lynden, Thomas accepted an offer from Mr. Hart to go with him through a seldom visited part of the country. The travelers started from Somerset on March 25, with a Hottentot attendant. Riding across extensive plains, they found themselves passing through herds of springbok, which along the banks of the Little Fish River became so numerous that an estimate suggested they could view twenty thousand at one time. Thomas recorded that as the horsemen rode over the plains these animals verified their name by springing away with graceful leaps.

As yet Thomas had not seen elephants, but this trip took him through their country. He was, accordingly, constantly on the watch for these great animals—yet with no wish to see them too close, for the African elephant is huge, powerful, and unpredictable. Unlike his relative of India, who can be completely domesticated, the elephant of Africa is truly of the wilds, never deigning to accept captivity. Though Thomas did not see the animals themselves, he was able to observe some of their work. He immediately realized that he, Mr. Hart, and the Hottentot guide would never have traversed the country beyond the Zureberg without the "roads" created by the movement of elephants passing through a mass of evergreens and succulent plants, such as milkwood, spekboom, and euphorbia, reaching to a height of almost fifty feet. Even with the help of the elephant roads and the experience of Mr. Hart and the Hottentot guide, they lost their way in the maze and barely escaped being caught there during the night. Despite the desire Thomas had to see elephants, he did not wish to meet them in the dark and at such a place. Just before night they emerged from this dangerous area and finally reached their destination, Enon, without harm. Here Thomas made a determined effort to find a herd of elephants which he could observe, but all he was able to find was stories of what they had done. He seemed always to arrive just too late to see them; so, for the present, elephants had to remain in his imagination.

When he started across the country with Mr. Hart, Thomas made note of the changes in the land before them. The phrases which he used in his account show the variations as they passed before his eyes.

[As the riders started out, the observer from Scotland recorded that] . . . we pursued our journey over extensive plains . . . and undulating heights, clothed with a brown and scanty herbage . . . the country became still more waste and dreary. . . . At length, after a toilsome ride of about fifty miles, during the latter half of which we had not found a single fountain, or pool, or running brook, to assuage our burning thirst, we reached about sunset the hovel of a Dutch-African boor, on the side of a rill that gushed, cool and limpid, from a savage-looking chasm of the Zureberg; the mountain towering overhead in precipitous crags. . . . [Now the scene shifts.] The summits of the ridges were often almost flat, and covered with long, coarse, wiry grass, of the sort called *sour* (whence the names *Zureberg* and *Zureveld*); being of such an acidulent quality that sheep and cattle will not eat it without great reluctance . . . [From grass he turns to mountains.] the mountains before us became more lofty and desolate, and the rugged path . . . more intricate and difficult. We were forced frequently to alight, and to lead our horses, or drive them before us, through the rocky defiles, and along the dangerous brink of precipitous declivities. Descending the gorge of a rocky ravine, we then penetrated, as it were, through the bowels of the mountain, following the windings of a narrow but verdant glen, adorned with occasional clumps of copsewood and forest trees, and enlivened by a brawling rivulet. . . . At length this little stream entered a yet wilder chasm among the rocks, where the foot of man or beast might no farther accompany it, and we were forced again to ascend the mountain ridge. . . . On the left, a billowy chaos of naked mountains, rocks, precipices, and yawning abysses, that looked as if hurled together by some prodigious convulsion of nature, appalled and bewildered the imagination. [Next, a panoramic view is given] . . . This was the fore-ground of a vast but sombre landscape. Before us, and on either hand, extended, far as the eye could reach, the immense forest-jungle which stretches from the Zureberg even to the sea-coast at the mouth of the Bushman's River. Through the bosom of this jungle we could distinctly trace the winding course of the Sunday River . . . not from the course of its waters, but from the hue of the light-green willow-trees . . . which grow along its margins. Beyond, far to the south, appeared the Indian Ocean and the shores of Algoa Bay . . . we descended . . . and entered the verge of the forest which spreads half-way up its skirts. [A movement is now made from a position where long views were possible to a place in which only very short ones could be obtained.] We entered . . . an alley, made by the elephants. . . . It was about six feet wide, and arched over, like a summer alcove; for the elephant, forcing his way through the thickets, tramples down or breaks off the larger branches that obstruct his passage, while the lighter and loftier, yielding to the pressure of his huge body, meet again like a Gothic arch when the monarch and his troup have passed through.[7]

At this time in Thomas Pringle's experience with Africa an intense interest in the physical aspects of the country through which he traveled was a natural one. Yet the physical scene was never more than a part of his concern. On his next journey, July, 1821, Thomas went with his friend Mr. Hart into the Albany district, where most of the English settlers had located. He examined the kind of housing they had provided for themselves and observed the manner in which the premises were kept. His practical farming sense immediately directed his attention to the soil of the area, and one paragraph in his journal would have been of almost inestimable value to the 1820 Settlers before they left England.

> In travelling over the open plains and savannahs, we found very generally a light sandy soil of grey, yellow, or blackish hue, upon a clayey bottom. . . . The herbage, though abundant, was almost universally of the description called *sour,* and consequently not very suitable for sheep; but varying much in quality and appearance in different situations. The quality of the soil, likewise, varied very considerably . . . except under the woods, it appeared generally much more meagre than the alluvial soils of the upper country. . . . The want, moreover, of fresh water in some places, and the precariousness or brackish quality of many of the brooks and fountains, together with the impracticable character of the river banks, and the poverty of the soil over a large extent of the more open country, appeared to present formidable obstacles to the existence of a dense population, or of a very extended agriculture; and rendered no inconsiderable portion of this much-lauded district unavailable for any other purpose than the pasturage of horned cattle and horses.[8]

For some years, little but frustration and suffering followed the settlers who went into the Albany district, and soon Thomas Pringle was to write about the conditions under which they were working. Through his efforts the people in England and Scotland were to learn much of what was happening to their relatives thousands of miles away in South Africa. Though the settlers had to contend with problems other than soil and climate, many of their ills started with these elements.

V *Elephants and then Cape Town*

Before Thomas left his family for Cape Town, he was successful in finding a herd of elephants—fifty-three he counted and concluded there were others not seen. Riding with a group of officers and talking about the great animals which he had not met, Thomas noticed something moving over the top of a bush close to the party. He cried, "Look out there!" and as they rounded the bush, the little group found itself less than a hundred paces from an enormous male elephant, estimated by some of the officers to be fourteen feet in height.[9] The elephant did not attack, and later the whole herd was discovered. At last Thomas Pringle had experienced African elephants at home, something which words seem unable to convey to a mind which has not encountered an actual meeting.

After more than two years with his family at Glen-Lynden, Thomas finally received the summons for which he had been waiting. The governor had appointed him to a place in the newly created South African Public Library, now beginning its life in Cape Town. Though he had sought no specific type of employment from the government, nor a particular town in which to settle, the young author must have felt that at last his academic training and literary experience were going to be given congenial surroundings. Yet nothing that he had seen or heard since the *Brilliant* entered False Bay prepared him for what waited beneath Table Mountain.

CHAPTER 3

What Happened in Cape Town

DURING July, 1822, William, the eldest son of Robert Pringle, with his family and relatives from Scotland, reached Glen-Lynden. There he settled upon the farm which Thomas had been holding for him, and now the younger brother, who for two and a half years had been official head of the party, felt that his obligations were fulfilled. It had been his stated desire to see his family united in rural independence. This had been accomplished. The Pringle party, which had emigrated on the basis of a grant of eleven hundred acres, now held twenty thousand. Though much of this land had not been occupied and stocked, the Pringles had made progress during their first two years. Houses had been built, crops such as wheat grown and harvested, gardens developed, herds and flocks started, roads built, and servants obtained. The Pringles were established and beginning to feel at home. Though Thomas had worked hard and successfully for his father, brothers, and sisters, it would be a mistake to assume he had neglected his own future. Both his mind and journal were filled with information which would soon begin to appear in magazines and later books. Even now, knowing that he had been appointed to the library, Thomas did not hasten to Algoa Bay to sail for Cape Town. Instead he elected to travel—this time with his wife and her sister—by land, more than five hundred miles. Obviously, he was still collecting data, though as yet he probably did not know what he could do with his information.

After a visit at Somerset Farm, where John Pringle was agricultural superintendent under Mr. Hart, the small party started its long journey on August 17, 1822. On the third day they reached Graaff-Reinet, which Thomas speaks of as "a handsome country town" of some two thousand inhabitants. Graaff-Reinet lay at the southern base of the "Sneeuw Bergen" and on the edge of the Great Karroo. Water was brought in a canal from the

Sunday River to the settlement on the edge of the desert. Writers both before and after Pringle expressed admiration for the garden which had been created in this arid spot. Here the party remained for several days, finally starting for Cape Town on August 23, in the company of Jacob Maré, his wife, and two daughters. Because the drought in the Karroo was more serious than normal, the group ascended the Sneeuwberg and passed along its ridges for a considerable distance. At this elevation, despite the cold, there was water and pasturage. Accepting what proved to be erroneous information, the party descended the Sneeuwberg and essayed a crossing of the Karroo along the Kareega River. For two days the absence of water was complete, and the party retreated to the edge of the desert and pushed toward the village of Beaufort, which they reached at the end of August. On September 3 they left Beaufort and started to cross the Karroo along the course of the Lion's River. During the first day, Thomas counted the skeletons of thirty-two oxen, recent casualties along the route. For four days they moved through this region without seeing a human dwelling and few living creatures. They were unable to attain more than fifteen miles a day—much of that after dark. On September 7 they reached the home of a man named Nel, where a fountain gave water to men and oxen. For four days the country beyond this fountain was much the same as before it. Late at night on the second day, they rested in the channel of the Rhinoceros River. The bed was covered with blue sand, but there was no running or standing water. By digging they obtained enough of what might be called water to furnish a scanty supply for the next two days, where for forty miles there was not a drop. About midnight on September 11 they heard a running stream and knew that the land of death was behind them. With dawn they saw a green landscape. In this country of vegetation they could secure fresh oxen and move toward Cape Town. Five days later, September 17, after frigid hours in the darkness on the heights, they descended to the glen of the Hex Rivier, Witch's River, and gazed upon "elegant and capacious dwellings, skirted by orange groves, vineyards, and corn-fields, and by extensive orchards, with the peach and almond trees covered with blossoms." [1] Now, in reversal, they were detained two days by the flooding Hex and Breede rivers. The party reached Cape Town on September 25, 1822. Except for one excursion, Pringle was to remain in Cape Town from this time until February 11, 1825.

I *A New Start and Defeat*

Living in Cape Town was more expensive than in Edinburgh or London, and Pringle understood that he would need to supplement his income from the library, which was paying him only seventy-five pounds sterling a year. The hours, 9:00 A.M. to 4:00 P.M., made only certain types of additional employment possible. Quite naturally he turned to teaching. Though good academic instruction was desperately needed in the city, the day at the library made it difficult for him to offer many hours as a teacher. Almost immediately he wrote to Scotland and begged his friend John Fairbairn to sail for the Cape. There was no reply. Only when Pringle explained that he felt the Cape needed and wanted a magazine and that he and Fairbairn were the men to start it did he get a reaction—this time instantly. Fairbairn wrote, March 2, 1823, that he would arrive about six weeks after his letter. He reached the Cape on October 10, 1823, but before that time hope for a magazine had been destroyed. Though it was obvious that both men wished to write and all they needed was a place for publication and pay for their work, they now turned to the school as a source of income. On November 18, they addressed the governor for permission to establish a classical and commercial academy. The request was approved, and the academy was started December 1, with Fairbairn in charge of instruction.

With little doubt, 1824 was the most eventful period of Thomas Pringle's life. The previous year had been one of preparation. Early in 1823 Pringle and the Reverend Abraham Faure decided to ask the governor for permission to start a "South African Magazine," the English edition by Pringle and the Dutch by Faure. Somerset heard of their plans and sent an unofficial message suggesting that he was opposed to the undertaking. Not to be stopped, Pringle and Faure presented their memorial on February 3. Lord Charles made no reply but wrote a letter to England in an attempt to learn the view of Earl Bathurst, secretary of state for the colonies. Meanwhile, the colonial secretary advised the "editors" that the governor had not been favorably inclined toward their project. Upon the very strong urging of the colonial secretary, the two men decided to wait. Months of waiting, however, killed their hope. Then, unexpectedly, Pringle was summoned by the governor and told that Earl Bathurst would permit the publication of a magazine. Pringle felt that Somerset gave the news with an ill-grace and insisted both for himself and Bathurst that nothing could appear that would be "detrimental to the peace and safety of the colony." [2]

Events were moving swiftly. One day Pringle and Fairbairn started their academy and the next they were told they could start a magazine. Quickly, on December 20, they issued a preliminary announcement. Abraham Faure was still a part of the venture, and on January 24, 1824, a longer prospectus was published in the *Cape Town Gazette,* explaining what the magazine would contain and saying that it would be published in alternate months, in English and in Dutch. The first number was announced for February and actually appeared March 5.

While Thomas Pringle and his associates were busy with plans for a journal, George Greig, a professional London printer who had arrived in March, 1823, announced on December 30 that he intended to start a newspaper, to be called *The South African Commercial Advertiser.* Greig, like Pringle, had sent a memorial to the governor, requesting approval of a weekly newspaper. There was no immediate reply, but in August he was informed that numerous such requests had been received and that they must be considered in order. Greig knew of no request except that of Pringle, but he now began to investigate another area of the question. He found that indeed there was a law prohibiting the publication without permission of journals and periodicals but that there was no law which forbade newspapers. Accordingly he moved at once to start his paper. The first number appeared on January 7; the second, on January 14. Popularity was immediate. At this time he approached Pringle and Fairbairn and asked them to become co-editors of his paper. They accepted, and soon the effect of their efforts could be seen in the quality of the publication.

After years of work and longing, Thomas Pringle must have felt that at last the right things were happening to him. His appointment to the library suggested a good start, and the academy was becoming a financial success. The newspaper was another source of income, and it offered a chance to write each week. The new magazine was about to be sent to press, and in this he would have both prose and verse. Dreams were rapidly becoming fact. All of this was brief, however, and began to disappear as it arrived. On March 5 Cape Town saw the first copies of *The South African Journal*, and the editors started work on the second number. Meanwhile, they were editing Greig's newspaper—where conflict with the government commenced.

Quite openely the editors of the *Advertiser* began to discuss the values of a free press in securing and preserving liberty. The attacks which they made upon despotism were clearly directed toward the government in general and especially Somerset. No one should have been surprised when the governor took the initiative away from the press. The fiscal, Daniel Denyssen, May 3, summoned Greig and told him that Lord Charles objected to certain articles and demanded ten thousand rix dollars' security against a repetition of the offence. Later the fiscal denied this charge. Greig returned to his office and wrote the fiscal asking for a detailed statement of his complaints and demands. The fiscal refused to put anything in writing. His subsequent move, May 4, was to order proof sheets of the paper before the next number was printed. When Pringle and Fairbairn learned of this, they refused to continue as editors. After the Government *Gazette* rejected publication of a notice of suspension of the *Advertiser*, Greig printed and posted handbills promising a statement of the facts connected with the censorship by the fiscal. Government men in the process of tearing these notices from Greig's own premises were stopped, and Greig demanded that the fiscal account for this action. Again the fiscal refused to give any written statement. About three o'clock next day, Sunday, May 9, the fiscal appeared with a warrant to seal the presses. He also had an order which banished Greig from the colony within one month. Though the presses were sealed, Greig refused to allow the sealing of the types because the warrant did not specify "types."

Not understanding the printing processes, the fiscal left thinking he had prevented publication of the "facts" promised the public. Greig now added to the "facts," which were for the most part already in type, a copy of the warrant, an account of the sealing of the presses, and the banishment order. The printers worked with mallet and planer all night, and Monday morning Cape Town was showered from an upper window with pamphlets revealing the whole story. Soon the fiscal appeared with authority to seal the types and even the doors to the composing room. His action had come too late. All Cape Town was aware of what was happening.

During the very hours of all of this action, the second number of *The South African Journal* was issuing from the press, May 7. It was Monday, May 10, that Greig scattered his printed "facts" across Cape Town. At 11:30 A.M., Thursday, May 13, a messenger from the fiscal came to the library and requested that Thomas Pringle come at once to the fiscal's office. When Pringle arrived, he found that official with a copy of the *Journal* before him. He said he was authorized to warn Pringle concerning remarks in the article, "On the Present State and Prospects of the English Emigrants." The governor, he said, felt that the editors had departed from the terms of their prospectus. He then required of the editors a pledge that nothing of this kind would happen again. Pringle declined to give the assurance asked. The next day he and Fairbairn sent a note of refusal and stated that the *Journal* was discontinued.

Having allowed himself several days to study with some care *The South African Journal,* the governor sent for Thomas Pringle, May 18. Whatever the intention of each man was as he moved toward this meeting, the two parted as absolute enemies. For Pringle, his place as an editor for Greig was gone with the sealing of the presses, and the *Journal* had come to an end with the letter to the fiscal. After this meeting, he resigned his position at the library. The "Literary and Scientific Society" in the process of being formed never became a reality. Soon pupils were being withdrawn from the academy, and before the end of 1824 Pringle had no resources left. On February 11, 1825, he and his wife sailed for Algoa Bay and returned to his family at Glen-Lynden.

II *The Struggle Between Pringle and Somerset*

History, not art, focused the crucial events of Thomas Pringle's life into a dramatic two weeks in May, 1824. Much that had happened and was happening in Europe was present in the room which held Lord Charles Somerset, governor of the Cape of Good Hope, and Thomas Pringle, editor, essayist, poet, that May morning as winter settled upon Cape Town. Here the old and the new met. As is often true, however, the conflict was not as simple as it appeared on the surface. In most ways, Lord Charles embodied the old, a civilization which was passing—which, in fact, in many ways had already passed. Here he was, though, thousands of miles from home and striving desperately to create a new country. The young man who opposed him was in his ideology very much a part of the thinking which had emerged from the French Revolution. Yet Thomas Pringle was in various ways part of the older world from which he had sprung.

If there is to be understanding of the situation, what needs to be stressed is that both men were in South Africa, not England or Scotland. It is necessary, therefore, to add something of the history of the Cape to the European background, which for most readers is much better known than events in South Africa.

Following the explorations of Bartholomew Diaz, who reached South Africa in 1488, and Vasco de Gama, who rounded the Cape in 1497, ships began to sail around the point. Vessels of the English East India Company became engaged in this trade as early as 1601, and in 1620 two English captains planted the flag of James I at the Cape. It was the Dutch East India Company, however, which in 1652 established a fort and planned for ships to take on not only water but vegetables and meat. The company at no time intended to accept the responsibility or expense of a colony. Their monopolies were complete and restrictions oppressive. Migration persisted, however, and the company's harshness merely drove farther inland those who had come to the Cape. This automatically began to develop the territory, which was the opposite of the company's intention. Development, though, proceeded in a very special way.

As the settlement in the Cape continued, each family became in principle a state—controlling its own territory, forming its own government, furnishing its own protection, providing its own education, regulating its own economy. Isolated in a primitive and hostile environment, these people conformed to the situation around them through absolute necessity. The boundary of what a family considered that it owned was determined by the extent of land which could be taken and held. All conduct was conceived at home, there being no authority outside or above the home. Protection was commensurate with the keenness of the eye, steadiness of the hand, strength of the muscles, calmness of the nerves, and courage in the heart. Education in any European sense became impossible—education being related to immediate practical needs—and the economy was first that of survival, next exploitation, and finally family-centered accumulation. Except for protection against loss from attack by the native tribes and wild animals, the setlers rarely considered the use of collective action.

Through the years increases in population made inevitable the creation of towns; for as soon as a family produced more than it could eat or wear or produced that for which it had no need, gathering of wealth depended upon trade. Everything that was done, however, was still under the control of a business organization. The area was not a state; so there was no government in a normal sense. Actions and reactions were shaped by the principle of profit.

Had the situation described here continued for a few years, the resulting influence might have been negligible. The whole area, however, was under this type of control for a hundred and forty-three years. It was in 1652 that the Dutch East India Company had established its station at the tip of Africa; on November 12, 1795, the governor and officers of the company left Cape Town with their families and property. They never returned. A quick recall will remind readers that in 1795 Europe was becoming quite busy with the activities of Napoleon. Actions and alliances in Europe, along with the presence of English ships and troops at the Cape, brought the area under the protection of England, at least for the duration of the present troubles. Passing from English control in 1802, the Cape was returned to the British in 1814, when the Prince of Orange and George III reached an agreement which, for six million pounds paid to the Netherlands, ceded the Cape in perpetuity to the English. Only six years after this beginning Thomas Pringle gazed through the early darkness trying to see the new land.

Writing in the middle 1960's, a South African author has speculated in the following way upon the history of the Cape before the coming of the English:

> It is strange to think that the fortunes of the Cape Colony were in general dictated by a group of business men who made no effort to promote the interests of the country from which they drew so great a benefit, or the men without whose presence and exertion their whole

half-way house scheme might well have collapsed. Speculation is staggered by how different the results might have been had the Company pursued a less selfish policy at the Cape. Its restrictive policy had a profound effect upon the Dutch Colonists with whom the English settlers were to come into contact in 1820, and, in view of the stultification of all progress, educational, spiritual, commercial, and agricultural, engendered by that Company, it is not surprising that the 1820 Settlers were to exercise such a great influence on the subsequent development of South Africa.[3]

> . . . Deprived for so long of some of the most fundamental privileges, these people [the Dutch] now found recognition of their needs, for Britain had embarked upon her great colonising enterprise and was prepared to grant privileges [to the Dutch] in return for loyalty and obedience. The provision of trade facilities, schools, churches, drostdies, improved communications and military protection [were offered].[4]

Above all else, the absence of a fixed boundary between European settlers and native inhabitants was the cause of both early and continuing trouble at the Cape. Waiving the whole question of right or wrong in various actions, at best a complex issue, the facts are quite simple but vastly significant. As already indicated, the East India Company welcomed the produce offered by the settlers but refused all responsibility for their existence. Thus the action of each emigrant was totally autonomous. As more and more arrived, movement inland was inevitable, but entirely on an individual basis. Shifts occurred for two reasons: to avoid the oppressive restrictions of the East India Company and to find more space and, if possible, better land. Each mile of expansion, however, involved the settlers in a conflict with the native tribes. Bushmen fought to the death, went into hiding and became harassers, or retreated to the desert areas. The little brown Bushmen, themselves famous hunters, were hunted by the Bantu as well as Europeans. In the eighteenth century smallpox had destroyed large numbers of the Hottentots and had cast as servants into the hands of Europeans many of those remaining. It was from the Bantu tribes, at the time all grouped under the word "Kaffir" (Pringle's "Caffer"), that great danger came. The Bantu seem to have originated near the center of Africa, had moved south along the eastern side of the continent, and had finally turned west. All of this represented some two thousand miles of migration by conquest. The end of this historical movement brought them into opposition with the South African Boers. Thus, when South Africa came into English possession, the government in London found itself with a serious frontier problem. The governor at the Cape, Lord Charles Somerset, suggested using emigrants to protect the eastern frontier. In 1817 his proposal was first considered in Parliament. Finally, in 1819, the House of Commons voted the funds which would send several thousand settlers to South Africa. Thomas Pringle was among these Settlers of 1820.

Few aspects of what existed in the Western world at the time were absent in the situation developing at the Cape. Lord Charles Somerset represented the belief in government by control from authority at the top. At this late period, however, the governor had not only the ancient obliviousness of, and disdain for, what would now be called "the people," but he distinctly possessed a more modern emotion, which perhaps should be identified by the word "fear." Somerset commanded and assumed that his voice was absolute, but on the fringes of his mental processes a persistent suggestion of a new world scratched. There were the American Revolution and the French Revolution as great lumps of evidence. Out "yonder" were "the people." Lord Charles had certainly not been trained to deal with them, but he knew that their existence had to be considered. One of the things he feared most was the press. Now that people could read, he understood the influence of the printed and distributed word. He was determined, therefore, to control the press at the Cape. Control of the press was the concept upon which Charles Somerset and Thomas Pringle were to disagree, and this disagreement brought them into public conflict.

Almost all that is known of Pringle establishes him as an opponent of Somerset. In him was the natural independence of the man whose family had lived on and from the soil for many generations. Emerging from this heritage, he had moved to the university and the field of literature. He had turned seriously to magazines and newspapers. Before he left Scotland, even if he had never sat in an editorial chair, he would have accepted as a normal process the free expression of ideas in the press.

Aware of the background of these two men, anyone can with ease predict the events which occurred. Pringle believed profoundly in the desirability of a free press while Somerset considered it extremely dangerous. Pringle was ready to do anything to maintain a free flow of comment, and Somerset was prepared to take any action which would keep all expression of ideas under his control. One characteristic completely absent from the life of Thomas Pringle was the spirit of compromise; conversely, Lord Charles Somerset was quite capable of compromise to get his way when force failed. As a final ingredient of the setting, it might be recalled that one man was born into an old and powerful family of England, the other was a lame son of an unknown Scottish farmer. When they met that morning in May, 1824, each man saw in the other what he hated. Thomas Pringle's account of the interview is one of the most passionate pieces of writing ever recorded by his pen. As he entered the governor's audience-room in the Colonial Office, Pringle says he found Lord Charles with the chief justice, Sir John Truter, seated on his right and before him was an open copy of the second number of the *South African Journal.*

. . . . There was a storm on his brow, and it burst forth at once upon me like a long-gathered south-easter from Table Mountain. "So, Sir!" he began—"you are one of those who dare to insult me, and oppose my government!"—and then he launched forth into a long tirade of abuse; scolding, upbraiding, and taunting me,—with all the domineering arrogance of mien and sneering insolence of expression of which he was so great a master—reproaching me above all for my *ingratitude* for his personal favours. While he thus addressed me, in the most insulting style, I felt my frame tremble with indignation; but I saw that the Chief Justice was placed there for a witness of my demeanour, and that my destruction was sealed if I gave way to my feelings, and was not wary in my words. I stood up, however, and confronted this most arrogant man with a look under which his haughty eye instantly sunk, and replied to him with a calmness of which I had not, a few minutes before, thought myself capable. I told him that I was quite sensible of the position in which I stood—a very humble individual before the representative of my sovereign; but I also knew what was due to myself as a British subject and a gentleman, and that I would not submit to be *rated* in the style he had assumed by any man, whatever were his station or his rank. I repelled his charges of having acted unworthily of my character as a government servant and a loyal subject;—I defended my conduct in regard to the press, and the character of our magazine, which he said was full of "calumny and falsehood"; I asserted my right to petition the king for the extension of the freedom of the press to the colony; and I denied altogether the "personal obligations" with which he upbraided me, having never asked nor received from him the slightest personal favour, unless the lands allotted to my party, and my appointment to the Government Library, were considered such,—though the latter was, in fact, a public duty assigned to me in compliance with the recommendations of the Home Government. This situation, however, I now begged to resign, since I would not compromise my free agency for that or for any appointment his lordship could bestow.

Lord Charles then saw he had gone a step too far. He had, in fact, misapprehended my character, and had made a not uncommon mistake, in taking a certain bashfulness of manner (*mauvaise honte*) for timidity of spirit. And as his object *then* was not absolutely to quarrel with, but merely to intimidate me, and thus render me subservient to his views, he immediately lowered his tone, and had the singular meanness, after the insulting terms he had used, to attempt to coax me by a little flattery, and by throwing out hints of his disposition to promote my personal views, if I would conduct myself "discreetly." He wished the magazine, he said, still to go on; and even alleged that the Fiscal had in some points exceeded his instructions in regard to us. But this attempt to cajole, when he found he could not bully me, disgusted me even more than his insolence. I saw the motive, and despised it: I saw the peril, too, and feared it: "timeo Danaos!" I resolutely declined, therefore, his repeated invitations (to which he called the Chief Justice formally to bear witness) to recommence the magazine, unless *legal protection* were granted to the press. And so ended my last conference with Lord Charles Somerset. I retired, and immediately sent in the resignation of my Government appointment.[5]

In a scholarly and perceptive consideration of the periodical literature of the Cape for this decade, Dr. A. M. Lewin Robinson has summarized the situation in the following paragraph.

While most of us may find it difficult, in an age in which greater freedom is allowed to the press, to approve of the government attitude in this matter and may admire the stand made by Pringle and Fairbairn, the fact should not be lost sight of that they had transgressed their self-imposed limits, firstly in the Prospectus attached to the Memorial to the Governor of February 1823, wherein the intention of "strictly excluding all topics of political or personal controversy" was declared, and the same sentiments reiterated in their later published statement of editorial policy in December 1823. When Fairbairn later told the Commission of Enquiry that he had never conceived that the introduction or discussion of political subjects was regulated by the conditions of any prospectus but only by the operation of existing laws, he was in no way strengthening his case. The Prospectus of 24 January 1824, as attached to No. 1 of the *Journal*, did certainly omit any mention of restriction of subject matter, but the Editors do state there that "their former Advertisement in the Cape *Gazette* of December 20th, 1823, renders it unnecessary for the Editors to go further into detail at present." It emerges then that while the fight for press freedom put up by Pringle, Fairbairn and Greig was both valiant and of great importance to South African history, they had little cause to be surprised at government censure, particularly in view of circumstances.[6]

Regardless of the right or wrong in the whole conflict, at that moment the governor possessed the power to create for Thomas Pringle an impossible economic situation. Thus, he and his wife soon were planning to leave Cape Town and return to the family at Glen-Lynden. Lord Charles had driven Thomas from the city, and in sligthtly more than a year he was to leave South Africa forever. Yet this was not the final act of the drama. History was with Thomas Pringle, not with Charles Somerset. The Dutch of the Cape were accustomed to treatment of the type displayed by the governor, but the newly arrived Englishmen were not. Back in England, Earl Bathurst had seen no reason for not permitting a magazine at the Cape. Then, too, the commissioners sent out at this very time to investigate Somerset's conduct of the government had said of Pringle's offending article in the *Journal*, "It can hardly be stated on a perusal of the article complained of, that the topics were controversially discussed, or if admissible at all, that the dissentient opinion of the writer could have been more moderately expressed." [7] The disagreement between Pringle and the governor concerned the "admissible at all" phrase. Though his prospectus had said he would refrain from consideration of this type of material, Pringle believed it should be discussed. Somerset insisted it should never be mentioned. The future was to say that Pringle was right and that Somerset was wrong. Though the little Scot left Cape Town in defeat, history has approved of his ideas and has preserved his name.

CHAPTER 4

Pringle's Publication Life at the Cape

BEFORE leaving Scotland, Thomas Pringle had not only seen his poems in periodicals but had published a volume deserving critical notice. This book, to be considered later in the present study, closed one phase of his life as an author. For three years his time would be filled with travel, hard physical work, and unusual actions. When he returned to print, his mind was filled with images and thoughts which before 1820 would not have visited him even in dreams.

I *Verse*

With the blank pages of a magazine now available, Pringle began to plan, write, and assemble some of the material written. Except for a brief lyric to his wife, "Wedded Love," completed before leaving Edinburgh [1] everything he offered his reader was written in South Africa, and only two compositions failed to treat of local material. One of these, however, was very closely related to current events at the Cape and so intensely a part of Pringle's nature that esthetic distance was impossible; thus, poetry was not the result. Before a reader passes beyond the title, he guesses something of what he will find: "*Verses,* On seeing in a late packet of English Papers, the Surrender of Cadiz, and the Proscription of a Free Press in Germany and Switzerland,—by Order of the 'Holy Alliance.'" There are twenty-one stanzas, dated February 1824. The ideological position taken by the author is stated directly in the first twenty lines.

Again we hear of distant wars,
  Of fields and cities lost or gained;
Of Kings and Emperors and Czars
  Colleagued to hold Mankind enchained.

We see a mean corrupted race,
  Of Monk and Profligate combined,
Resume again the Tyrant's place,
  And triumph o'er Man's soaring mind.

We see the hopes of Freedom crushed,
  All soiled the flag she late unfurled,
Her song upon the mountains hushed,
  And silent gloom pervade the world.

And one by one, each glorious light,
  Extinguished at the Despot's nod,
Expiring, leaves the wished-for night
  To clinch the chain and ply the rod.

Thus sink the stars in darkness deep
  When poisonous fogs usurp the sky,
And owls and vampires boldly creep
  Abroad–their villain task to ply.[2]

At this point the accusations become specific and names are used. In stanza eleven the speaker turns to England, "Whose beacon-light, 'mid Ocean set/ Impregnable—for ever burns/ To tell where Freedom lingers yet."[3] After calling a number of Englishmen by name, he utters the belief that "under Britain's guardian shield,/ Law, Freedom, Truth, [will] begin their reign."[4] Because his reaction to the packet mentioned could have been predicted with complete accuracy, the writing was almost certain to be propagandistic. Though it must be admitted that Pringle had more than slight precedent for his passionate directness, the method has seldom produced significant literature.

Likewise predictable was his composition of "An Emigrant's Song." The point of view is entirely usual, but some of the lines show him trying to suggest African characteristics, in phrases such as "howling waste . . . wild-beast roams at will . . . Savage lurks—to kill . . . adder's angry crest . . . growl from the lion's den."[5] It seems fair to suggest that the author was thinking of his audience at home, not his South African readers, because with one or two exceptions the claims of the poem are all very general. For readers in Scotland and England, however, the presence of adders, lions, and savages was quite enough to create a reaction without greater detail, especially when attached to the lament with which the song commenced.

By the lone Mancazana's margin grey,
  A heart-sick Maiden sung,—
And mournfully poured her melting lay,
  In England's gentle tongue:—

O! lovely spreads th' Acacia grove,
  In Amakosa's glen;
But fairer far the home I love,
  And ne'er must see again!

Far away is the land where my kindred dwell,
  And the home where my childhood grew,
And the scenes that of all my bliss can tell,
  When life and love were new.

Here, bright are the skies—and these vallies of bloom
  May allure the traveller's eye—
But all seems dressed in death-like gloom
  To the Exile, who comes—to die! [6]

With little doubt, the most interesting thing about "An Emigrant's Song" is the long note which accompanied it upon publication. The editors while ostensibly engaged in literary criticism seized the opportunity to comment upon the 1820 Settlers. In the second number of the *Journal* Pringle's article on the settlers was to be the basis for conflict with the governor. This footnote was in certain ways a prefatory statement.

The preceding Verses have been sent us by an esteemed Correspondent, and are among the most tolerable we have yet received from the English Settlements on the Eastern Frontier. But though not devoid of poetical merit, they are lamentably deficient in the more meritorious quality of manly and energetic determination. Virtue does not consist in the expression of amiable feelings, but in the active and persevering performance of arduous duties. The present calamitous situation of the Settlers may indeed excuse in some measure, (especially in a delicate female,) this despairing tone of sentiment; and we have admitted the Lines chiefly because they serve to indicate, aptly enough, the existing state of feeling among a large and estimable class of people. But this morbid tone of despondency, accords ill with the resolute and enterprising spirit of Englishmen. The Emigrants have suffered most severely; but we feel assured, that they are yet destined to surmount all their difficulties, and to finally succeed in South Africa, as Englishmen have always ultimately succeeded in every part of the world where they have once planted their foot. And, in token of this cheering result, we have pleasure in stating, that we have already received from the Locations, (though too late for insertion in the present Number,) several able contributions of a very different strain and tendency from the preceding;—being, at once, highly creditable to the persevering courage of the Emigrants, and calculated to convey to our countrymen at home, a much more pleasing (and we think a more just) impression of the general character of the country they have come to inhabit. Edit.[7]

Few notes have ever worked harder for the space used. Clearly, the editors were suggesting that they had received a number of verse contributions. If for no other reason than lack of time, this could hardly be true. Between the date of permission to publish and the appearance of the first number, there was only a brief period, and communication in South Africa was still slow, especially throughout the interior. In addition to lack of time, for the historian to assume much verse was being written on the frontier during these years would be ridiculous. Actually, Pringle as editor was writing of Pringle as poet. Thus there was no problem, looking either into the past or the future. In fact, while on the frontier, Pringle had started a very cheerful poem about his new environment: his house, food, himself, family, and friends. Written as if intended as a letter to Fairbairn, long before John left England for Cape Town, the lines were never sent. Completed in 1834, the poem was published in *African Sketches*.

Another achievement of the note was to allow a strong statement concerning the ills of the settlers, under the guise of exhorting them to fortitude and great effort. All of this was said in the process of praising the English, by an editor who was a Scot, not forgetting the governor was English. Finally, most of what was being written would have an effect both in England and at the Cape—not the same, but a valid and important one in each part of the world to which the observations were being directed. Certainly the note did its work well.

During April, 1821, only a year after he arrived in Africa, Pringle had on a trip with Mr. Hart visited the Moravian missionary establishment located in the valley of the White River, below the Zureberg. Interested in the passion for order which he found there and impressed by the work which he felt was being done for the Hottentots, he devoted some dozen pages in the *Narrative* to his visit and in addition wrote a sonnet, which seems to have marked the beginning of his South African poetry.

By Heaven directed—by the World reviled—
  Amidst the Wilderness they sought a home,
  Where beasts of prey, and men of murder roam,
And untam'd Nature holds her revels wild:
There on their pious toils their Master smil'd,
  And prosper'd them, unknown or scorned of men,
  'Till in the satyr's haunt and dragon's den
A garden bloom'd, and savage hordes grew mild.

So, in the guilty heart when heavenly Grace
  Enters—it ceaseth not till it uproot
  All evil passions from each hidden cell—
Planting again an Eden in their place—
  Which yields to men and angels pleasant fruit,
  And God himself delighteth there to dwell.[8]

Sentiments expressed in this sonnet are thoroughly normal for Europeans of the period. From a stranger's viewpoint Pringle has built the poem upon fact, and the whole has been shaped with economy. With very few words, the author establishes the situation. He speaks of the region in which the Moravians established their mission as "the Wilderness" because in the European sense it was almost totally uninhabited, and the land had never been cultivated. Too, as a European of recent arrival, he was constantly aware of the danger of wild animals and native tribes. Evidence of what could be expected from tribes in the area had been established when the missionary settlement was destroyed by the Kaffirs only two years before Pringle's visit. The missionaries had returned to their location and made a new start a few months before his arrival, this time with perhaps a better chance because one of the principal reasons for the presence of the 1820 Settlers was protection against Kaffir attacks. All of this part of the story is told or implied in the first half of the octet. In the second half, their success is stated and praised. The garden which bloomed was quite literal and became a source of food, though the use of satyr and dragon begins to pull the lines away from the literal. Making mild the savage "hordes"—the Christianizing of the Hottentots—was not the vast claim that would be suggested by the word today. Pringle regularly used "horde" in its original sense, referring not to *numbers* but to *nomadic* peoples. At times his context makes clear that the term refers to no more than a family, or tribal group. Here in the sonnet the total number of natives at Enon was about two hundred.

As the octave had prepared for the sestet, so the sestet looks back to the initiating statements. A felicitous example is the Eden "Which yields to men and angels pleasant fruit." The claim of the sestet is spiritual, but it parallels the physical fruit of the octet garden. The final line could not have been written by the author in obliviousness of the story of God's walking with Adam in the Garden of Eden. Thus, the sonnet maintains balance between the direct and indirect, the specific and the general.

Only a few hours after going ashore at Algoa Bay, in May, 1820, Pringle had gone into the interior a short distance and begun his acquaintance with the native people of South Africa. When he and his party started for their location on the first night, he recorded in his journal his impressions of natives traveling with the group. Now in the first number of his magazine he attempts a poem, "Caffer Song," which purports to be a native woman's singing of her home in the deep woods beside the Grey Rock. Though the location is actual and the singer's mind is filled with native images, the diction and rhythm of the lines are thousands of miles away among the author's beloved Scottish glens.

Only two of Pringle's poems were used in the second, and as it proved last, issue of the *South African Journal*, of May, 1824, but "Afar in the Desart," which first appeared here, is the poem that almost alone created the author's reputation. Since it was frequently reprinted and went through a number of revisions, in the present chapter identification of some of the motivating experiences may prove more appropriate than other approaches.

Because the first two lines of the poem are repeated four times and because they have remained unchanged since the time of initial publication ("Afar in the Desart I love to ride,/ With the silent Bush-boy alone by my side:—"),[9] the images presented are perhaps the most easily identified among all he used.

Starting with his early school days, Thomas Pringle had seen the environment around him from the back of a horse. When he finally stood upon the South African soil of Baviaans River, he realized that his first requirement was guard from attack by natives and protection against the weather. After that he needed a horse. Two facts pointed toward the requirement: there were no roads, and there was always his lameness. Thus few men have ever seen from a horse so much of the Cape as Thomas Pringle. Upon his first short trip from the beach at Algoa Bay, he had a native beside his horse. Of this initial ride he recorded, "A Hottentot boy . . . acted as my guide, and trotted along at a goodly pace by the side of my pony."[10] Upon the first excursion out from Glen-Lynden, Thomas noted that he had no apprehensions about the trip, "Being now mounted . . . on the light and hardy horses of the country, with an active Hottentot lad for a guide. . . ."[11] Pringle's first extended trip was made half a year later, but he still refers to "a Hottentot attendant. . . ."[12] While at Enon, wishing to survey extensively the White River country, he "started one morning before sun-rise, and set out on horse-back on an exploratory ramble, accompanied by a Hottentot guide on foot. . . ."[13]

Though in his movements about the Cape Pringle had seen and remarked upon many barren or waste areas, crossing the Karroo he had experienced hours he was never likely to forget. In the fifth stanza he names the Karroo, specifically, but those who have followed Thomas through his various wanderings are likely to feel that the author directed the attention of his readers to any waste area, not merely the famous Karroo. Thus, within the poem, one has the feeling that he intends not only the specific but the general also.

Into three middle stanzas, the author introduces much of the wild life of South Africa. He names the Deer, Buffalo, Oribi, Nhu *(sic)*, Gazelle, Hartebeest, Gemsbok, Eland, Elephant, River-horse, Rhinoceros, and Wild Ass; the Springbok, Zebra, Ostrich, Vulture, Wolf, Jackall, and Hyaena *(sic);* the Snake, Lizard, and Bat. Along with the wild life, he mentions the poisonous thorn, bitter melon, and the Salt Lake. For a poem of a hundred lines, there is more than enough of this kind of material to allow the author to display what he had encountered as he moved about the Cape.

With mention of the Karroo and "Wilderness vast," Pringle describes "A region of emptiness, howling and drear. . . . Where grass, nor herb, nor shrub takes root. . . . A region of drought, where no river glides. . . . But the barren earth, and the burning sky. . . ." [14] Here were images some of which became standard in South African poetry. Pringle's sky burned on into the twentieth century.

Very different from anything else that he had written was "The Lion and the Camelopard," [15] the last of his poems to go into the *South African Journal.* These lines were printed immediately after the second of his articles on "The Lion." Close readers will have noticed that both the lion and the giraffe (camelopard) were absent from the long list of animals in "Afar in the Desart." It appears that the author was saving his favorites for a separate poem. Whether or not this theory is correct, at the end of his second article on lions Pringle concludes with a statement which directs the reader's attention to the poem printed on the next page, lines concerned with these animals: "To the Verses that follow it may be a sufficient introduction to mention, that I was informed by the Bechuana Chiefs, that the Lion occasionally surprises the Giraffe or Camelopard in the manner here described; and that, owing to the amazing strength and fleetness of that magnificent animal, he is sometimes carried away *fifteen* or *twenty* miles before it sinks under him. This fact, I believe, has been formely mentioned by travellers, and has been ridiculed as absurd by European critics. But the soothfast evidence of my friend, Old Teysho, the wise and sagacious Vizier of great Mateebe, Autocrat of all the Bechuanas, is sufficient for me; and will doubtless be allowed its due weight, when the matter is again discussed by the Scavans of Paris and Edinburgh." [16] Whatever the reason for its composition the work represents a very important development in South African poetry. Though "The Lion and the Camelopard" is not a good poem, it shows a writer who was born into the eighteenth-century tradition of elegance attempting to present a realistic account of the attack of a lion on a giraffe. The literary attempt fails because the diction and rhythm were totally unsuitable for what Pringle was trying to create and because in endeavoring to get close to the battle he lost all esthetic distance, as he allowed the reader to become exposed to raw flesh and blood. As a writer he as yet did not understand how to create what an impulse was telling him to achieve. Despite the immediate failure, however, Pringle had as early as 1824 *published* a poem which attempted to create a piece of literature using in a naturalistic way materials from the South African wilds. Almost a hundred years would pass before writers of the Western world discovered, or perhaps rediscovered, how to get very close to material of this type and yet impose the kind of form that would not destroy but make literature of the substance employed.

II *Prose*

Four prose pieces were used by Pringle in the two issues of the *South African Journal.* The two articles on "The Lion" were signed T. P., the one on the "Zureveld" identified as from a journal (his own) written in 1821.[17] The account of the present situation of the 1820 Settlers was written as an editorial. What Pringle had to say about the lion was the beginning of a series "On the Character and Habits of Some of the Wild Animals of South Africa." The description of the Zureveld was orientation for the later discussion of the condition of the English emigrants. Obviously in a conscious and systematic way Thomas Pringle was beginning to use the information stored in his mind and the notes recorded in his journal.

When a reader finishes Pringle's lion stories, he sighs with regret that the *South African Journal* abruptly ended its life and thus never printed the elephant stories promised next. Writing neither as a scientist nor as an expert of any kind, the little Scot had merely collected stories about lions and lion hunts, which he now related quite effectively. Prose did not intimidate him as poetry did. He seems to have had no fear of simplicity, concreteness, and a direct approach to his material. With no suggestion that he was following any literary theory, he trusted the facts about lions, the events witnessed or received from competent sources, and the meaning implied by what was related. He had delivered everything into the reader's mind and assumed that there it was safe. He was correct, and the result was quite satisfactory.

With only the slightest suggestion of an interest in organization, he devotes only three lines to the classification of these animals in South Africa and moves immediately, as a very poor scientist but a good storyteller, into an Africa which immediately begins to exist for the reader. His transition is made with ease. Because one type of lion is said to be fiercer and stronger, the author begins to tell of the beast's actions against the Bushmen. Everyone else hunted the Bushmen—Bantu, Boer, Settler—now the lion. Pringle makes his point quickly. The lions of the Bushmen territory are more fierce because the little brown people are not worthy opponents who would cause animals to fear and thus respect man. To eat a few Bushmen, even a whole family, was not great evidence of fierceness. From the eating of Bushmen the author passes on to stories of strength, lions carrying their kill long distances at high speeds. Soon he is defending the lion against charges of cowardice. Here he explains in detail how the animal's method of attack can be misinterpreted. His action against his foes leads to a consideration of the lion's attitude towards man. Pringle advances and defends the claim that the lion "appears to have the impression, that man is not his natural prey; and though he does not always give place to him, he will yet in almost every case abstain from attacking him, if he observes in his deportment neither terror nor hostility."[18] Making this claim inevitably leads to a discussion of the effect of the human eye upon that of the lion. Now begins a series of stories of encounters between the eyes of men and lions. From eye to eye stories, he slips without comment to confrontation accounts of various kinds, ending with an incident in which "Lucas van Vuuren, a Vee Boor," was saved when the lion decided to kill his horse rather than Lucas.[19] Returning to the site amid the safety of his friends, Lucas was furious with the lion, not for eating the horse but for stealing the saddle, for which the Vee Boor gravely insisted the lion could have no possible use.

Starting the second installment of his account of the South African lion with a discussion of the general opinion that the great beast preferred to eat black men rather than white, Pringle questioned at once the "Cape Boors" explanation that it was a choice between "Christian *men*" and "Hottentot *folk*."[20] Pringle insisted that it was scent which led the lion to one rather than the other, and his examples support the claim.

Now the author concludes his article with several stories which fit no category, though two end with a comic rather than a tragic climax. One he had been told in the Cradock district; the other happened to himself and the Scots at Glen-Lynden. In both, man had sought out the lion, who upon extreme provocation had charged. In each instance all had escaped except one man. In the first episode, the helpless man decided that it was prudent "to lie flat and quiet as a log. The victorious *Leeuw* snuffed at him—scratched him with his paw—and then magnanimously bestriding him, sat quietly down upon his back. His routed companions, collecting in a body, took courage at length to face about; and, seeing the posture of affairs, imagined their comrade was killed, and began to concert measures for revenging him. After a short pause, however, the lion resigned of his own accord his stool of triumph, relieved his panting captive, and retreated towards the mountains. The party, on coming up, found their friend shaking his ears, unharmed from the war—except what he had suffered from a very ungentlemanly piece of conduct in the lion, who it seems had actually treated his prostrate foe in the same ignominious sort as Gulliver did the palace of Lilliput on a certain occasion—and for which he was afterwards justly impeached of high treason." [21]

Much that was best in Pringle, along with some of his weaknesses, as a prose writer and narrator is displayed in his account of a lion hunt arranged by the Scottish settlers at Glen-Lynden. One night in 1822 a lion had killed the favorite riding horse of Thomas himself. Without taking time to send for neighboring "Dutch Boors," the nearest being twenty miles, the Scots started out with their "Bastaard Hottentots." The enemy was located and the standard harassment begun, but the lion declined to lose his temper.

. . . . At length after some hours spent in thus beating about the bush, the Scottish blood of some of my countrymen began to get impatient, and three of them announced their determination to march in and beard the lion in his den, provided three of the Bastaards (who were superior marksmen) would support them, and would follow up their fire, should the enemy venture to give battle. Accordingly in they went, (in spite of the warnings of some more prudent men,) to within fifteen or twenty paces of the spot where the animal lay concealed. He was couched among the roots of a large evergreen bush, with a small space of open ground on one side of it; and they fancied, on approaching, that they saw him distinctly, lying glaring at them from under the foliage. Charging the Bastaards to stand firm and level fair should *they* miss, the Scottish champions let fly together, and struck–not the lion, (as it afterwards proved,) but a great block of red stone–beyond which he was actually lying. Whether any of the shot grazed him is uncertain, but, with no other warning than a furious growl, forth he bolted from the bush. The rascally Bastaards, in place of now pouring in their volley upon him, instantly turned, and fled helter skelter, leaving him to do his pleasure upon the defenceless Scots, who, with empty guns, were tumbling over each other in their hurry to escape the clutch of the rampant savage. In a twinkling he was upon them, and with one stroke of his paw dashed the nearest to the ground. The scene was terrific! There stood the lion with his foot upon his prostrate foe, looking round in conscious power and pride upon the bands of his assailants,–and with a port the most noble and imposing that can be conceived. It was the most magnificent thing I ever witnessed. The danger of our friends however rendered it at the moment too terrible to enjoy either the grand or the ludicrous part of the picture. We expected every instant to see one or more of them torn to pieces:–nor, though a band of us were standing within fifty paces with our guns cocked and levelled, durst we fire for their assistance. One was lying under the lion's feet–and the others scrambling towards us in such a way as to intercept our aim upon him. All this passed far more rapidly than I have described it. But luckily the lion, after steadily surveying us for a few seconds, seemed willing to be quits on fair terms; and with a fortunate forbearance . . . turned calmly away, and driving the snarling dogs like rats from among his heels, bounded over the adjoining thicket like a cat over a footstool, clearing brakes and bushes 12 or 15 feet high as readily as if they had been tufts of grass; and, abandoning the jungle, retreated towards the mountain.[22]

As a comment, Pringle records the reaction to this lion hunt of the local Boers. "Our neighbours, the Nimrods of the Tarka, disapproved highly of our method of attacking this lion in the bush, and said, it was a wonder he did not destroy a few of us. They were highly amused with the discomfiture of our three champions; and the story of 'Jan Rennie en de Leeuw,' still continues to be one of their constant jokes against the Scotchmen. This is all fair—and it forms a just counterpoise in favour of our good humoured neighbours, when the Scottish farmers quiz them too unmercifully about their uncouth agriculture and antediluvian ploughs and harrows."[23]

Pringle's Publication Life at the Cape

From lion stories, Pringle passed to an extremely serious consideration of the state in which the 1820 Settlers found themselves during the early months of 1824. Since his own family at Glen-Lynden was in an incipient period of success and he felt at ease about their future, he was free from personal concern in that area. There were in Cape Town, however, few so completely prepared or eager to discuss the problems of the 1820 Settlers as Thomas Pringle. Not only had he sailed from England with them and started life on the frontier but he had traveled, observed, and asked questions throughout the territory.

Now he was ready to speak, and the more perfectly pre-prepared he was to discuss the subject the less welcome would his observations be to Lord Charles Somerset, who was under pressure from England to account for conditions at the Cape. Naturally wherever a speaker or writer touched the situation he was raising political questions. Despite all of his disclaimers, Pringle knew this. In his initial paragraph, he explains that the first number of the *Journal* had carried no discussions in "minute detail" because the Commissioners of Inquiry from England were present and engaged in their investigation. This having been completed, he now advanced the opinion that "The public have now a right to know something of the matter; and it becomes our duty, as Journalists, to discuss the subject candidly and deliberately, upon general grounds; and to afford whatever aid we can, to make it perfectly understood, before any new arrangements are undertaken, either by the Government or by the Settlers themselves." [24] Few even in 1824 would have objected to this theory. Weaknesses lay not in the idea but in its execution. Implicit in Pringle's phrases is the assumption that theory and practice will be identical. Quick to point to the fallibility of rulers (and rightly), he left unnoticed the fallibility of journalists. The weakness, of course, is human not occupational. Human beings need restraints, but Pringle as much as Somerset rejected all opposition. When Thomas refused to be restrained by the governor, Lord Charles destroyed the editor's position in Cape Town. His writing, however, remains and now after generations can be examined and evaluated.

Going about his work in a systematic manner, Pringle considers the "present state" of each group of settlers; those still on the lands assigned to them, those who have moved to the town and assumed positions as mechanics, others who have accepted hire as laborers, and finally a few small special classifications. He is also systematic in discussing the differences between such groups in the Cape as the wine producer, corn grower, and stock farmers. He lists general causes of failure in a one, two, three, four order. He not only knows facts, but he understands how to organize materials.

Weakness reveals itself when he shifts from fact to theory, when he begins to state what might have happened if certain things had been done. Stating that one of the reasons for the emigration plan of 1820 was the "engrafting of a British upon the Dutch population," he tells his reader that "The advantages arising to the Cape from a steady influx of British Settlers, would have been immense. The free spirit, which Englishmen inhale with their earliest sentiments, would have accompanied them, and defused [*sic*] itself by degrees through the more apathetical and lucre-loving Dutch, until it leavened the whole mass, and communicated a public spirit, such as Britain is proud to acknowledge in all her legitimate offspring. The intimate connection between the Emigrants and their Mother Country, would have excited a more lively attention in England towards the Colony, and a more watchful regard in her Government to its interests. The English habits and more numerous wants of the Settlers would have been gradually communicated to the rest of the Inhabitants, and would have established a far more considerable and constant demand for English produce. The continual influx of free labourers would have compensated the Colony for the diminishing value of Slave labour, and have speedily rid us of that abomination, without expense, injustice, or danger; whilst the enterprise and activity of the British Emigrants would have diffused themselves throughout the whole of our Colonial population, continually discovering new articles of produce, more profitable branches of industry, new channels of commerce, new resources against natural evils, and better remedies for artificial ones." [25]

Writing a sentence such as "The free spirit, which Englishmen inhale with their earliest sentiments, would have accompanied them, and defused itself by degrees through the more apathetical and lucre-loving Dutch, until it had leavened the whole mass, and communicated a public spirit, such as Britain is proud to acknowledge in all her legitimate offspring," Pringle seems to have believed he was making the same type of claim that may be seen in a sentence which says, "The breed of wool-bearing sheep, which the 1820 Settlers were promised in the earliest announcement of plans for emigration, would have accompanied them to the Cape, and diffused the breed, through the area among the less productive types used by the Dutch, until flocks were improved and excellence attained, such as Britain is proud to acknowledge in all of her wool-growing parts of the world." Even in this situation, reservations should be made. A new breed of sheep might die in a strange climate, just as the Cape wheat crops of the 1820 Settlers had been destroyed by rust. The final result might be total failure. Pringle, however, who could ask and follow advice in building houses, planting crops, developing orchards, even hunting lions, had absolute confidence in the correctness of his concepts when they turned toward the political, social, religious. In his initial paragraph, he had said that "it becomes our duty, as Journalists, to discuss the subject candidly and deliberately . . . to make it perfectly understood." Here it may be urged that "perfectly" makes demands which are beyond human nature. Perfection does not exist concretely and in fact, but only in certain types of mind. Seemingly, practical physical details could exist in Thomas Pringle's mind beside vast abstractions without either ever bothering to turn to the other and acknowledge its presence. For this reason, Pringle in his prose usually was at his best when he felt he was attempting least.

CHAPTER 5

In the Name of Humanity

THOUSANDS answered Parliament's 1819 call to sail for the Cape. Early the next year a fleet transported some four thousand hopeful men and women to South Africa. With confidence, they landed at Algoa Bay and moved inland to occupy the land which the government assigned to them. Arriving at the beginning of winter, they had time to build shelters and prepare soil for planting as spring approached during the late months of 1820. Crops during 1821 were a failure. Along with other problems, *rust* had appeared in the wheat. Failure the first year was followed by the same result the second and the third years. Many were forced to leave the land, and most of those who remained were in desperate circumstances. In Cape Town a group was organized to aid in relieving the distress. Expectation of help from England also seemed natural. Though Pringle was not in an economic position to contribute money, he gave his time and everything his pen could do for the settlers. A tragic climax came in early October, 1823, when a destroying storm moved through the area in which the emigrants had located. Little was left to the settlers except life, and many were thankful to have retained a hold upon earth itself. Now Thomas Pringle the humanitarian sought the assistance of Thomas Pringle the writer who possessed practical experience as a settler. Soon a book was on the way to London. A letter dated January 5, 1824, begged the publisher, Thomas Underwood, to make every effort to see that these pages were printed as soon as possible.[1] Underwood did his part, and *Some Account of the Present State of the English Settlers in Albany, South Africa,* appeared in 1824.

Despite all of the pressure under which publication was being arranged, Pringle's preparation had been thorough and the manuscript he sent to England was not a hastily sketched document. His part in the undertaking was greater in fact than in theory.

According to his own printed statement, he had merely "prefixed a short description of the country" to indicate that success was still possible; actually, he wrote an introduction of forty-nine pages for a book which ran to little more than a hundred. The conclusion was likewise Pringle's, and the remainder of the volume was a collection of letters from writers who either lived in the area being considered or were experts, such as Mr. Hart of Somerset Farm, making visits of inspection. Everything possible was done to establish the accuracy of claims and thus demonstrate the need for relief. Though the first half of the book was far less dramatic than the letters which told the story of the destructive storm and the desperate condition of the settlers, the pages Pringle contributed were from the first moment of value as a guide into the whole situation and have remained relevant as a part of the history of the time and of the place.

Certainly one of the problems Pringle had to consider was the vast difference between the country the settlers found and the one they had expected to find. The lack of agreement between accounts of the country arose from that which was written by those Pringle calls "tourists" and the trained practical observer with time for careful examination. He says early writers described the Albany district as "a fair and fertile region of unrivalled beauty and fecundity;—extending in luxuriant plains to invite the plough-share, or swelling into verdant hills, which only wanted flocks and shepherds to be quite Arcadian;—adorned, moreover, with evergreen groves and forests, and with the superb and glowing allurements of euphorbias, strelitzas, chandelier aloes, and scented acacias;—its lawny solitudes enlivened by sportive herds of elegant antelopes; and the whole landscape embellished (as they usually express it) 'with all the picturesque scenery of a nobleman's park in England'; but rather, as transmitted through this 'pictured medium,' like a landscape in fairyland." [2] Pringle accepted the kind of error presented here as a natural one, but he suggests that the effect in England was extensive and serious because potential emigrants acted upon these false impressions. He comments:

> I do not mean to attribute any great blame to the travellers and tourists for their tempting descriptions; for the Zuureveld is really a pretty country, and to persons passing hastily through it, who had no ac-

quaintance with agriculture or the peculiarities of the soil and climate, it could scarcely fail, in favourable seasons, to display a very alluring aspect, and to call forth encomiums far too unqualified. It would have been fortunate for the emigrants, doubtless, if they had listened more sceptically to such accounts; and if persons who could look farther below the surface, had been sent to precede them; or if practical information collected from the experience even of boors and Hottentots had been more carefully provided by Government. But the truth is, that the emigration to Algoa Bay was altogether too rashly and hurriedly concerted. A sort of Utopian delirium was somehow excited at that time in the public mind about South Africa, and the flowery descriptions of superficial observers seem to have intoxicated with their Circean blandishments, not merely the gullible herd of uninformed emigrants, but many sober men also both in and out of Parliament.[3]

Upon this reaction, Thomas, his brothers, and his father could comment with considerable feeling, for they were among those who had accepted the accounts to which he now refers. In the present book, however, Thomas makes it clear that his plea for help does not include a request for assistance to his own family. In their mountain valley, they were already beginning to succeed. Part of Pringle's faith in the whole venture must have come from his intimate knowledge of what his father and brothers had done and the present results of their efforts. He knew where others had made errors and therefore understood how their mistakes could be corrected. His belief in the project was not an easy optimism but a position reached because of hard work and careful attention to detail. With assurance it can be claimed that Thomas Pringle had lived the method used to present for his reader the situation in the district of Albany.

Looking across the area as he had first seen it, Pringle presents the reader with the whole region before he begins to examine details. The territory included some two thousand square miles, known as the Zuureveld or Zureveld. Little time, however, is devoted to the general scene, and the author moves quickly to a consideration of particular problems. He explains that the many rivers which have cut deep channels on their way to the Indian Ocean make almost impossible east-west travel by wheeled vehicles. Also movement close to and parallel to the rivers is made difficult by the numerous "gullies or kloofs, choked up with thorny copsewood, that run down to the deep channels of the rivers from the plains on either side."[4] This leaves only the area between streams and at some distance from the channels. Travel by horseback was, obviously, the most expeditious method available.

Early writers had called attention to the large numbers of great wild animals in the area, but Pringle assures his readers that the numbers have been greatly reduced. The number of animals was of practical consideration to the settlers. Lions, for example, were always dangerous; elephants, destructive; springboks, fond of young corn. Nature had solved their problem for those who wished to be farmers or graziers.

Logically, Pringle now proceeds to an examination of the nature of the soil available to the settlers. Though living before the time of scientific analysis, Pringle's knowledge of farming prompted him to note all of the visible facts. He was aware of both the surface and subsurface soil, the nature of what was already growing on the land, the quantity and quality of the water available. He observed that the soil varied from point to point within the general area. This fact was relevant in deciding what type of farming or nonfarming would be suited to each part of the whole. Thus, he could reach an estimate of how many settlers the whole territory would support. In all of this he was aided by what he had learned with his family at Glen-Lynden and by the fact that during his investigation he had the advice of Mr. Hart, from the government farm at Somerset.

While examining the soil and vegetation of the fields he viewed, it was natural for Pringle to observe and comment upon the houses the settlers had built for themselves. Two of the facts he had noted in 1821 became evidence of crucial weakness when a great storm came in October, 1823. Pringle wrote that most of the settlers had built houses not likely to wear well or stand against severe weather. Also serious was the fact that they had often built below marks which indicated previous high water from storms. When this was called to their attention, they seemed unimpressed. After they knew how wrong they had been, it was too late.

Very carefully Pringle distinguishes between errors which could have been avoided and which might still be compensated for and difficulties which could not have been foreseen. The sudden appearance of *rust* in the wheat was something the settlers could not have anticipated because before 1820 there had been little of this destroyer in South Africa. Now for three years the wheat was damaged or completely destroyed by *rust*. Yet even in an area of this kind, Pringle felt that eventual control would come and success would replace failure. With the usual practical sense of his family, he notes that "solid stem" wheat seems less subject to *rust* than the variety then being planted and thus would provide one way of adjusting to the situation. He observes that barley is attacked by *rust* less often than wheat and that Indian corn, South African mealies, appeared almost immune. In this and many other ways, Pringle shows that aid to the settlers is not merely to cover failure and thus relieve human suffering but to promote final success and thus independence—a word he used more than once in relation to what his own family was attempting in its new home.

Turning to how the settlers had been redistributed because of conditions, Pringle begins to focus upon human needs and make his plea for help from "home." Because many of the original settlers had left the land, the requirements to provide for those remaining would be less than might be supposed. Here is how Pringle presents the situation as it appeared in 1824.

This remnant of the English emigrants (probably not now much exceeding one third of their original number) consist chiefly of the heads of parties, and of independent families who expected to establish themselves on their several allotments by the aid of their own funds, or the exertion of their own industry. These two classes have been by far the most unfortunate, if not the exclusive sufferers, by the result of the emigration. The mechanics and labourers found sufficient and profitable employment on the locations, so long as the funds of the superior settlers lasted; and, for the first two years, received also, in many cases, the public rations, even without working at all. And it must be confessed, that owing to the latter circumstance, along with other causes, that naturally tend to spoil servants in new colonies, a good many of this class, and other ill-selected emigrants, have conducted themselves with much reprehensible idleness, improvidence, and presumption. A few individuals of this description may probably still be found on some of the locations, or lingering about the *canteens* (or *brandy shops*) of Bathurst and Graham's Town. But the great body of the labouring settlers, whether of this, or of a better description, gradually abandoned the settlement, and quietly dispersed themselves throughout the colony in the manner above mentioned, when the means of their employers had failed, and the free rations and local restrictions were alike withdrawn by the colonial government. And it cannot be doubted that this will ultimately lead to beneficial results both for themselves and the community. The price of labour, amidst all the calamities of the colony, continues high and unabated. Three rix dollars (or about five shillings sterling) per day, with provisions, is the usual wages given to mechanics, and nearly half that amount to common labourers. With such encouragements there can be little question that these classes have generally improved their condition by emigrating; and if any of them are *now* distressed (unless under peculiar circumstances), it may be presumed, without breach of charity, that they deserve to suffer, and ought not to be inconsiderately relieved.[5]

Having handled with directness the situation in relation to the mechanics and unskilled laborers, Pringle turned to those for whom the book is in fact being written.

But the settlers left on the locations are under very different circumstances, and have (as a body) very different claims to the public sympathy. They were men of some property and of adventurous spirit, who came out under an agreement with their mother country to colonize an important position in the Cape settlement. They have made zealous and persevering exertions to effect that object, but have been depressed by unforeseen obstacles, and overwhelmed by a continued series of unsurmountable disasters. They were mistaken, many of them, doubtless, in giving credit to too flattering accounts of the character and capabilities of the country; but not more culpably mistaken than the Government, that partly countenanced these accounts, and sent them to colonize it upon an injudicious and ill-concerted plan. They have exhausted their strength and resources in prosecuting the impracticable task assigned them, of rendering the Zuureveld exclusively an agricultural settlement with a dense English population. And though the meagre soil and precarious climate of Albany were amply sufficient to baffle that attempt, yet they might possibly, with the support of a liberal government, have retrieved, in some measure, their prosperity, by turning their attention more to pasturage, upon some system of extended allotments, had not Providence seen it meet to afflict them with four successive seasons of unprecedented failure in the crops, and crowned their calamities by the late destructive storm or hurricane. Their means are now utterly wasted, and their spirits quite depressed and broken. Their lands, hitherto almost unproductive and altogether unsufficient in extent, are moreover mortgaged to the colonial government for the stores and rations formerly supplied, and more recently in some cases, as I understand, for money advanced to relieve their extreme necessities. And although in these and other respects a liberal and generous conduct will doubtless be pursued by the colonial office, yet it is evident, that if something far more decided and efficient be not done for them, both by the Government here and by the public at home, the inevitable ruin of the most respectable and meritorious portion of the emigrants, and of the English settlement in general, must be the speedy and melancholy consequence. For although every bond and burden on the original grants were cancelled to-morrow, and the full rights of property delivered to them free of expense, what could they possibly effect on their present allotments, or even on grants sufficiently extended for pasture-farms, without funds to purchase herds and flocks, or to provide herdsmen and shepherds to guard them? A few individuals of superior rank and resources, such as Major Pigot and two or three others, may indeed be able to surmount their accumulated losses, to keep their followers together, and to yet reach a state of independence, unassisted. But, unquestionably, the great mass of even the educated and superior settlers are now altogether destitute of any such resources; and if not promptly and effectually assisted, must soon succumb under their misfortunes, and gradually sink, with their respectable families, into irretrievable pauperism and spirit-crushing squalid destitution.[6]

Having separated those who required help from others who did not and having made clear the urgent need of the settlers who had remained on the land, Pringle began to consider the future of those he seems to have assumed would be aided by both government and private means. He points out that the reduction of the number of settlers offers an immediate advantage in a new distribution of land. Now it will be possible without moving to a new location to offer a family three thousand acres where they had occupied one thousand. In addition to the lands made available because of abandonment, other areas originally allotted to the Highland Scots who never arrived might now be used. Pringle suggested that the territory intended for the highlanders was in many ways superior to the Albany district. Regardless of the relative merits, the two together would supply sufficient land for the diversity which was needed. Soil suitable for crops could be farmed, but that which was not could be profitably diverted to grazing. Even this much choice would, Pringle insisted, make it possible for the settlers to survive. Being assured of a hold upon the territory, the settlers could then initiate experiments in an effort to discover what else they could do to increase the range of production and thus reduce danger of serious loss because of the failure of any one thing at a given time.

Recommending that the settlers move into the highlands meant proximity to the Kaffir border, with its obvious danger. It was in this area that Thomas had lived with the Pringle family, and now he expresses his opinion concerning the defense potentialities of the Cape.

> Though on such subjects I would wish to offer my own opinion with much humility and deference, I cannot repress a strong conviction, formed during a residence of two years on that frontier, and confirmed by frequent conversations with experienced officers, who had long served on it, that the Caffers may be effectually checked, and their predatory inroads completely repressed or prevented, by establishing a line of small posts or fortified villages along a well-chosen frontier, and communicating with each other by constant patrols. Nor would any increased military establishment be necessary for this purpose. A native militia of *free Hottentots,* to whom should be given an interest in the soil as a reward for their services, might be entrusted with this charge (for which of all men they are the best fitted), and be rendered the prosperous and permanent occupiers of this advanced line of territory. Behind them might be placed British settlers (with a few hundred Highlanders among them if possible), the whole being covered and supported by small garrisons of regular troops and Cape cavalry in the strong fortified posts of Fort Beaufort, Fort Willshire, and the Beka.[7]

Moving toward a conclusion, Pringle compares the hardships and dangers of life in South Africa with the situation in other countries, such as New South Wales and Canada. It is ultimately the South African sun that wins, and he decides that there is no reason to leave the Cape seeking a better land. Along with the climate and other things, he has kind words for the Boers and the Hottentots, both of whom he knew well. As he compared advantages with disadvantages, he could see no reason for the 1820 Settlers to leave South Africa. Pringle must have felt that his own family was proving this position correct, and he believed that others would certainly succeed.

Despite all of the immediate practical reasons which prompted Thomas Pringle to write *Some Account of the Present State of the English Settlers in Albany, South Africa,* a reader soon begins to feel that the author is doing more than making a humanitarian appeal, though he certainly performed his appointed task well. In these pages, however, he reveals something about himself. His interest in the Boers and the Hottentots shows that the people of South Africa are becoming important to him in a very personal way. When he speaks of the Boers, he is not thinking of a group but of the individuals who had extended hospitality to him, given valuable information, and demonstrated courage, sound leadership, and admirable human integrity to the young Scot who had approached them as a stranger with questions and doubts. Likewise, his observations about the Hottentots developed from his experiences with them from his earliest days at Glen-Lynden. Perhaps the ultimate importance of all of this is that slowly but quite certainly South Africa is becoming a part of Thomas Pringle and that when he sails away he will take much with him back to England.

CHAPTER 6

Both Scot and South African

WHEN early in 1824 Thomas Pringle sent to London the manuscript in which he discussed the present state of the 1820 English Settlers in the Albany district, his expectations in South Africa were high. All of his projects were already successful or promised to succeed. Yet before the end of the year, everything had failed. On October 8 he started with W. T. Blair and Captain W. Miller to visit the Albany settlements and the chief mission stations between. Riding through Stellenbosch and over the Franschehoek (also Franschhoek and French Hoek) pass, the little group reached Genadendal, a Moravian mission, on October 11. Here they remained for the night and were some seven or eight miles on their way the next morning when a dog from a Boer's house rushed out and frightened Pringle's horse, throwing Thomas to the ground and fracturing his lame hip. Carried back to Genadendal, he was there attended by Brother Stem, but professional medical aid could not be made available for two weeks, when it was too late. Margaret arrived from Cape Town, and though having her was a comfort nothing could change the fact that the accident took still another half inch from his lame leg. By the middle of December, Thomas was well enough to travel, and he and Margaret returned to Cape Town and began to settle their affairs in preparation for leaving. Though they sold everything possible, they were still too deeply in debt to think of returning to England. Consequently, Pringle sold his books, and he and Margaret sailed for Algoa Bay on February 11, 1825. Their object was to return to his family at Glen-Lynden, where he still had some land and a few sheep and cattle.[1]

Back on the frontier, Pringle wrote to Fairbairn in a tone rarely seen in his published work. "I have spent a couple of weeks in setting my house or rather hut in order—in putting my desk & table together & manufacturing bedsteads chairs & cutting stocks.

My mechanical talents I am happy to say are still unimpaired—& my cottage & furniture are the admiration of the Bavians River. They even greatly exceed the grandeur & magnificence of my former state. Beside my own exquisite handiworks I even possess an iron bedstead & a cane-bottomed sofa. In short I am a very great personage & my influence & reputation (in spite of my loss of court favour) are equal to my magnificence. I am patriarch priest & king. I have Boors for Clients & Bastaards for vassals. I have set afoot a Sunday School & perform services every Sunday in Dutch to an audience of about fifty souls—who come in waggons & on horseback, male & female—old & young—the black Chivalry of the Bavians River." [2] This mood, however, was temporary. Soon an extreme restlessness began to fasten upon him, and he rapidly moved toward an attitude which would take him back to England and into the work which would consume most of the few years permitted to him. Before the end of 1825, Thomas and Margaret were perparing to leave the Cape. They had gone down for the last time from the Baviaans River valley to Algoa Bay. With the help of funds from friends in Cape Town, they sailed, probably on the brig *Luna* on April 16, for England, arriving in London July 7, 1826. Thomas had remained on African soil two weeks less than six years.

When Pringle came to London, he found little to encourage him. Help presented itself, however, from a natural source. In January, 1826, before leaving the Cape, he had written an article on the state of slavery in South Africa. This was published by T. Campbell in his *New Monthly Magazine* for October. The ideas and information brought Pringle to the attention of the Anti-Slavery Society, and they offered Thomas the position of secretary. He assumed his duties in March 1827. Although the salary was only about two hundred pounds a year, it was the beginning of a chance to make a living. The work was, of course, in complete harmony with his innermost nature and deepest principles. If peace could exist in such a man, Thomas should now have been at peace with himself—if not the world—and could begin to consider his destiny. This meant serious thoughts about his place in the literary world. Soon after he began his work with the Anti-Slavery Society, he assembled all of the poems (as is usually said) that he wished to keep among his collected works and in 1828 brought out a volume of more than two hundred pages. The book contained most of *Autumnal Excursion,* published in 1819, just before he left Edinburgh for the Cape, and South African poems which had resulted from the six years in his adopted home. The new book was called *Ephemerides;* or, *Occasional Poems, written in Scotland and South Africa.* Already the process of selection, revision, and rearrangement is in progress. Though as yet far from complete, the work has advanced to a point at which serious criticism can begin.

I *The Romance of Scotland*

When in 1828 Thomas Pringle focused his attention upon the poems which had formed his first book in 1819, for obvious reasons he gave "The Autumnal Excursion" some of the prominence and honor accorded it as the title poem of his early collection. With the exception of "Afar in the Desart," at the time perhaps no other poem that Pringle had written meant quite as much to him as this one. Not only was it directly connected with one of the dearest of his early friends, Robert Story, the youth with whom he had attended the university, and connected the poet with the country where he was born and the scenes he learned to love as a boy, but this poem also was his first to receive significant recognition. These lines had brought him to the attention of Sir Walter Scott, who had also attended Kelso Grammar School and pronounced the village to be "the most beautiful if not the most romantic . . . in Scotland." [3] As is normal, however, in poems of this type, far more attention is given to local history, events the author wishes to remember, and personal reaction to the countryside than to any serious attempt to present the region itself. Much, in fact most, of the poem is thoroughly conventional. The question to ask is, What did the author do with the conventional elements he inherited?

Writing in tetrameter couplets, Pringle shows skill in his ability to relax the rigid form.

Dear S. . . . .; while now the south ern breeze *a*
Floats, frag rant, from the up land leas, *a*
Whis pering of Au tumn's mel low spoils, *b*
And jo vi al sports and grate ful toils,— *b*
A wake ning in the soft en'd breast *c*

Re grets	and wish	es long	sup prest,—	*c*
O, come	with me	once more	to hail	*d*
The scent	ed heath,	the sheaf	y vale,	*d*
The hills	and streams	of Tev	iot dale.[4]	*d*

Though this passage has few subtitutions for the foundation meter, the metronome beat in relation to duration and stress within the words creating feet showing the same technical markings reveals the source of the actual rhythm of the passage. Thus, while the iambic pulse is always present, there is enough variation to avoid much metrical monotony. Most of the monotony in the poem arises from the rhyme scheme, and even here the young poet is working hard to secure a graceful flow.

One of the identifying characteristics of the tradition within which Pringle was here writing was the use of a constant procession of adjectives.

Cayla! like voice of years gone by,
I hear thy mountain melody:
It comes with long-forgotten dreams
Once cherish'd by thy wizard streams;
And sings of school-boy rambles free,
And heart-felt young hilarity!
I see the mouldering turrets hoar
Dim-gleaming on thy woodland shore,
Where oft, afar from vulgar eye,
I loved at summer tide to lie;
Abandon'd to the witching sway
Of some old bard's heroic lay;
Or poring o'er the immortal story
Of Roman and of Grecian glory.[5]

In the passage here quoted the author is employing an average of more than an adjective per line, in short lines. How much this is a part of the tradition into which he was born will be seen by observing the following collection of sample lines, taken from authors of the half century immediately preceding Pringle. "The shelter'd cot, the cultivated farm. . . . And drowsy tinklings lull the distant folds. . . . Night, sable gooddess! From her ebon throne. . . . From the rude mountain, and the mossy wild. . . . Along the glimm'ring walls, or ghostly shape. . . . By winding myrtles round your ruin'd shed. . . ." [6]

While the formal aspects and diction of the lines fitted comfortably into its period and place, the poem presented a record of much that was very dear to Pringle as an individual. Of considerable importance is the section which offers one of the few published references to his mother, who had died when Thomas was six. Now, in his first attempt to write a major poem, he remembers her in the following way:

> Ah, while amid the world's wild strife
> We yet may trace that sweeter life,
> Now fading like a lovely dream,—
> Why cannot memory too redeem
> The glowing hopes, the thoughts sublime,
> The feelings of our early prime?—
> Alas! like hues of breaking day
> The soul's young visions pass away;
> And elder fancy scarce may dare
> To image aught again so fair—
> As when that Mother's warblings wild
> Had sooth'd to rest her sickly child,
> And o'er my couch I dream'd there hung
> Celestial forms, with seraph tongue,
> Who told of purer, happier spheres,
> Exempt from pain, unstain'd with tears—
> Or when I woke, at midnight deep,
> When heaven's bright host their vigils keep,
> And view'd with meek mysterious dread
> The moon-beam through the lattice shed—
> Deeming 'twas God's eternal EYE,
> Bent down to bless us from on high!
>
> And when that gentlest human Friend
> No more her anxious eye could bend
> On one, by young affliction prest
> More close to her maternal breast,
> I deem'd she still beheld afar
> My sorrows from some peaceful star,—
> In slumber heard her faintly speak,
> And felt her kiss upon my cheek.

And oft, when through the solemn wood
My steps the schoolway path pursued,
I paused beneath its quiet shade
To view the spot where she was laid,
And pray like her's my life might be
From all ungentle passions free,—
Like her's, in pain or sorrow's hour,
My hope and stay that holy Power,
To whom, even 'mid delirium wild,
Her prayer consign'd her weeping child! [7]

These lines about his mother, here given without either the introduction or conclusion, were entirely appropriate in a poem devoted to the celebration in a very personal way of Scotland, of the southern highlands, of the scenes he had known as a child. Seldom, however, in the rest of the poem does the author create images so specific as, for example, the one in which he speaks of pausing between home and school to see his mother's grave. Normally the type of writing being attempted in "The Autumnal Excursion" moves towards generality, even in remembering personal experiences. The passage in which Pringle describes the scenes of his childhood, though filled with place-names, gives only general images, except for readers who know intimately the places persented. It is probably not irrelevant to speculate that the impulse which originally created this type of poem assumed it would be received only, or for the most part, by those who knew the places and events depicted. Thus, the following lines are developed upon a foundation of proper nouns with the addition of a selection of common nouns and modifiers operating at a high level of abstraction:

Then, let us roam that lovely land,
By classic Teviot's sylvan strand,
Paternal Yair and Plora's glens,
And haunted Yarrow's "lonesome dens";
Till, with far-circling steps we hail
Thy native Beaumont's broomy dale,
And reach my boyhood's birchen bowers
'Mong Cayla's cottages and towers.[8]

While no poet has composed what might be identified as a great piece of writing of the kind that Pringle has attempted here, it was a very good point from which to start. The verse is competent, the phrasing graceful, and the sentiments proper. With considerable force the effort demonstrated that the young author could sustain over a span of thirty pages the level he had set for himself. This first poem in the volume convinced the reader that it would be wise to examine with care the rest of the book.

Though "The Autumnal Excursion" had required the first thirty pages of *Ephemerides,* the remaining twenty-one poems of Scotland needed only forty-five pages. Ten of these poems were sonnets, seven songs, and the other four of different types. This distribution immediately suggests two things: Pringle was following in form the tradition into which he was born rather than attempting anything original, and he had already acquired some range. Almost everything in this volume suggests the author was conscious of the methods used to become accepted. Despite the fact that it could not have given him much, either economically or in reputation, he was writing songs. In a note he explains: "The following Songs were mostly written for old unpublished Scottish airs; and inserted, along with the music, in Mr. Alex. Campbell's 'Anthology,' in 1817–1818." [9] One of the values to the young writer was the practice it gave in learning to control form. In composing seven songs, he employed seven different stanza patterns, from four lines to eight. He also availed himself of the chance to engage in metrical variation. Certainly it was valuable as exercise work, and a few samples will show what he was achieving.

> O fresh is the breeze of my mountains,
>   When morn lifts her bright dewy eye;
> And pleasant my birk-shaded fountains,
>   When the fervors of noontide are high;
> And lovely the hour when the grey-mantled gloaming
>   Adown the dim valley steals softly along,
> And meets me alone, by the far forest roaming
>   To watch the first notes of the nightingale's song.[10]

> I hate Ambition's haughty name,
> And the heartless pride of Wealth and Fame;
> Yet now I haste through ocean's roar
> To woo them on a distant shore.[11]

My cheek has lost its hue,
My eye grows faint and dim;
But 'tis sweeter to fade
In grief's gloomy shade,
Than to bloom for another than him! [12]

And Edward, Scotland's deadly foe,
Has pledged my captive hand
To him—who wrought my kindred's woe,
And seiz'd my father's land! [13]

O fragrant was the bower
Of the hawthorn in flower,
And the wild-briar rose just blowing,
When I parted with my love,
In Glen-Garva's birchen grove,
And we plighted our vows ere going,[14]

My hawks around the forest fly,
And wonder that I tarry,
While lone on thymy banks I lie
And dream of dark-hair'd Mary!
O sweet is she who thinks on me,
Behind yon dusky mountain;
In greenwood bower, at gloaming hour,
We'll meet by Morag's Fountain.[15]

Tempests may assail us
From Affliction's coast,
Fortune's breeze may fail us
When we need it most;
Fairest hopes may perish,
Firmest friends may change;
But the love we cherish
Nothing shall estrange.[16]

While passages from the songs display technical competence and suggest the author was capable of handling particular types of material, little of what Pringle might become in an African setting was revealed. It is in the sonnets that a reader is first given some feeling for what may happen at the Cape. Here, more than once, the Romantic haze is abandoned, much of the inherited diction is set aside, and specific experience becomes not only the motivation but is actually projected. In the first sonnet of the 1828 volume, he proved that he could remember his youth, refer to the ancient stories of Scotland, talk about poetry, and at the same time offer a poem which was simple, direct, and effective:

> They call'd us brother bards: The same blue streams
> Witness'd our youthful sports: our tears have sprung
> Together, when those ancient tales were sung
> That tinged our fancy's first and sweetest dreams–
> Two simple boys bewitch'd with magic themes!
> And still as riper years and judgment came,
> On mutual couch we plann'd our mutual schemes,
> Our tastes, our friendships, and our joys the same.
> But not the same our task: Thy venturous lyre,
> Which with the tide of genius swells or falls,
> Shall charm tumultuous camps and courtly halls,
> And rouse the warrior's arm and patriot's ire–
> While I shall chant my simple madrigals
> To smiling circles round the cottage fire.[17]

Starting with the form of the Italian sonnet in the first quatrain, the author has made the second quatrain English; then he returns to the Italian for the sestet. The rigidity of the Italian rhyme scheme, however, is jolted by the full stop in the middle of three lines; and, of course, the failure of line six to fulfill the normal expectancy. For a young writer who was founded in Latin, university trained, and certainly no rebel in the formal aspects of poetry, this is a promising piece of work. When South Africa received him, it was inheriting a trained poet and, from the above evidence, one capable of looking at an actual situation and converting the experience into a poem.

That Pringle was concerned with himself as a poet and also with other poets is exhibited more than once in the ten sonnets of the present group. At the end of the one just presented, he considers the kind of poet he is—or will become. Later in the group he writes a sonnet to honor the Scottish poet Thomas Campbell (1777–1844) and one in lavish praise of William Wordsworth (1770–1850). Wordsworth was finishing the best of his poems as Pringle was starting to write the first of his own. Pringle must have known Wordsworth well because as a university student he was said to be far more familiar with contemporary literature than was usual. In fact, it was quite clear very early that this young man wished to write, not enter any of the professions such as law, medicine, or the ministry.

How much Pringle desired to become a poet is clearly displayed in his efforts to write a poem ostensibly concerned with the supernatural—something still close to many people in his part of the world, even as the nineteenth century began. He had published the first version of this work in his 1819 volume, there called "The Isle of Eyra," only sixty-two lines, designated as a fragment. In 1828 the title had become "Fairy-land," and the lines increased to eighty-one, still only a minor effort, in fact merely the introduction to the final poem. Before consigning it to what became the collected work of his life, the author had expanded the fragment into eight times the length of the original. In its final form, called "A Dream of Fairyland," the poem is divided into six "Fyttes," each prefaced by one or more quotations. These passages attempt to guide the reader towards what he will find in each Fytte. A list of the authors quoted will give some understanding of what was being attempted. Fytte I was introduced by lines from Logan, Thomas the Rhymer, and Gawin Douglas. Then follow, for Fytte II Chaucer's *Dreame,* III and IV Spenser's *Faerie Queene,* V Milton's *Paradise Lost* and Wordsworth's *Laodamia,* VI Coleridge. The first fact which emerges from this list is that Pringle is proceeding chronologically. As might be expected, however, the time sequence becomes the basis for the developing idea of the poem. Fytte I, in the words of Thomas the Rhymer, starts out upon "the road to fair Elfland." Next, the dream comes from Chaucer, but in Fytte III, Spenser introduces a very different point of view. With Merlin of King Arthur's time, the reader is still in the world of magic, but the magic now has a deeply serious purpose, "to shew in perfect sight/ Whatever thing was in the world contaynd." Merlin's magic, then, was used to reveal what is usually called *reality* or *truth.* Then in Fytte IV Spenser is again employed, this time to associate the poet with what is revealed. Next, in the words selected from Wordsworth, the magic is dropped and the suggestion comes that it is possible to "Learn by a mortal yearning to ascend/ Towards a higher object." This power within mortal beings is described by Coleridge, Fytte VI, as "music in the soul," though Coleridge does not attempt to identify this music or give its source. Its identity and source remain a mystery, which means a return to an inability to explain, as with magic and elfland—but not a return to magic and elfland as now usually understood. Clearly, by the time Pringle completed his poem, all of the supernatural materials he used had become a literary method rather than a literal presentation. Thus, though at the end of the poem Pringle is still talking about the fairy world, he is now speaking of what the mortal world can learn from this "other world"; and though man can never attain the qualities of this fairy region, he can view it, and the implication is that man may be guided by what has been experienced. It is quite clear, also, that Pringle is thinking in religious terms as much as fairy terms. Thus, at the end, he writes:

> Hung my listening soul upon
> Words (which I may not rehearse
> In this vain and idle verse)—
> Things with deepest meaning fraught
> By that Gentle Fairy taught,
> In whose mien I then might trace
> The sister of man's godlike race,
> Ere his half-angelic nature
> Lapsed into the lowlier creature,
> Ere the golden link was riven
> That upheld the heart to heaven,
> And the ethereal light grew dim
> Of the fallen seraphim!
> —Lovely lessons *there* I read,
> There I learn a lofty creed,
> In the expression of a mind
> By a fearless faith refined,
> Such as we of mortal strain
> Beneath the stars may not attain,
> But such themes are all too high
> For this lay of Phantasy;
> So I close the rambling rhyme
> Of my Flight to Fairy Clime.[18]

Despite the disclaimer, there seems little doubt that Pringle takes seriously some possible link between the natural and supernatural worlds, especially when the supernatural world becomes heaven. In "The Autumnal Excursion," he recorded that he and Robert Story had sat upon the tomb of some of Pringle's ancestors and considered at length "man's mysterious mortal state." [19] Then a few lines later he observes quite directly, "I love to think/ There still may last some mystic link/ Between the living and the dead,—/ Some beam, from better regions shed,/ To lighten with celestial glow/ The pilgrim's darkling path below. . . ." [20] This attitude he appears to have held to the end of his life.

None of the three remaining poems which belong to the group written in Scotland is a major effort. The wild flowers from the fields and woods Pringle had known in his youth composed "The Wreath" for Mary, "simple Nature's sweetest child." [21] Another poem, "Azla," is a search for his "favourite Maid," [22] characterized by images from the natural world. In "The Legend of the Rose," [23] he tells the story of how the rose received its thorns. Though written with grace, these poems add nothing to the poet's stature, nor do they damage his reputation.

II *Lines from the Cape*

Having established his poetic reputation with "The Autumnal Excursion," Pringle undertook something of a parallel to this in his first South African collection, with "Evening Rambles." Though the later effort was much shorter and far less ambitious, it attempts to present, as the early poem had, a natural setting connected with the writer's life. Both poems are distinctly in the same tradition, employ the same verse form, and often are very close together in tone. Perhaps the most important difference is that the later poem presupposes a different relationship to its audience than that assumed by the early composition. As Pringle wrote about the South African mountains and valleys which had recently become home, he certainly believed that his audience was a European one—thousands of miles away and ignorant of this new environment. In Scotland, myth, legend, history, and experiences of childhood and youth were not only present but dominant. Now it is the natural scene that controls the composition. Under this influence, the description at times becomes specific enough for a reader to feel the presence of an actual scene, though the lines—or most of them—are still guided by the methods that Pringle had inherited. The following passage, for example, reveals the greatest distance the author travels from the tradition in which he developed:

Sterile mountains, rough and steep,
That bound abrupt the valley deep,
Heaving to the clear blue sky
Their ribs of granite, bare and dry;
And ridges, by the torrents worn,
Thinly streak'd with scraggy thorn . . .

Yet, where the vale winds deep below,
The landscape wears a warmer glow:
There the spekboom spreads its bowers
Of light-green leaves and lilac flowers;
And the bright aloe rears its crest,
Like stately queen for gala drest;
And gorgeous erythrina shakes
Its coral tufts above the brakes . . .

And now, along the grassy meads,
Where the skipping reebok feeds,
Let me through the mazes rove
Of the light acacia-grove; . . .
And the duiker at my tread
Sudden lifts his startled head . . .[24]

Identification of the audience for which Pringle was here writing lies in his use of notes to give the scientific name for all of the flora and fauna of this poem—and other poems. Only through notes could the author tell a European reader what he was seeing when he gazed toward "spekboom," a "reebok" or "duiker." These and many others were normal Cape names, and Thomas Pringle used them without self-consciousness. Yet he was considerate of readers not from South Africa.

Despite the introduction of local names, "Evening Rambles" does not convince a reader that he has sailed very close to the Cape, much less that he has moved inland and is viewing the Baviaans River valley. Another composition, however, from the same place and time, brings one much closer. In the first stanza, a reader of "The Lion Hunt" hears the call to assemble and quickly will learn where the men go and what they do.

Call Arend and Ekhard and Groepe to the spoor;
Call Muller and Coetzer and Lucas Van Vuur.

Ride up Skirly-Cleugh, and blow loudly the bugle:
Call Slinger and Allie and Dikkop and Dugal;
And Gert, with the elephant-gun on his shoulder;
In a perilous pinch none is better or bolder.

In the gorge of the glen lie the bones of my steed,
And the hoofs of a heifer of fatherland's breed . . .

Ho! the Hottentot boys have discovered his track—
To his den in the desert we'll follow him back;
But tighten your girths, and look well to your flints,
For heavy and fresh are the villain's foot-prints. . . .

By mountain and forest, by fountain and vlei,
We have track'd him at length to the coverts of Kei.

Mark that black bushy mound where the bloodhounds are howling;
Hark! that hoarse sullen sound like the deep thunder growling;
'Tis his lair—'tis his voice!—from your saddles alight,
For the bold skelm-beast is preparing for fight.

Leave the horses behind—and be still every man;
Let the Mullers and Rennie advance in the van;
Keep fast in a clump;—by the yell of yon hound,
The savage, I guess, will be out with a bound.[25]

As one might guess, the more than a dozen names in this part of the poem given are all real and the hunt actual. The important fact here, however, is the ease with which South African words are assimilated. No one is likely to argue that this is a significant poem, *in any sense,* but it is historically valuable. Here writing was a poet with European ideas and style which belonged to the time and place of his birth, but these lines proved that the materials and language of this new country could and should be used. Because it was impossible to put Pringle aside as an unsophisticated local writer, he was accepted both in Europe and South Africa. His influence at the Cape was considerable and of long duration. This does not mean South Africa immediately produced poets to fill Pringle's place when he sailed away in 1826. It did not. Yet the physical absence of the author did not mean the absence of his work. With the publication of *Ephemerides* in 1828, South Africa acquired the beginnings of a literature in English.

In addition to his use of names, setting, and actions belonging to South Africa, Pringle turned toward the native inhabitants for materials. He did more, however, than employ the natives as subjects for description. In a thorough and systematic way, Thomas Pringle established a specific point of view. It was this method which created the basis for his influence, and even today few readers can examine a group of these poems and remain indifferent to the ideas expressed. Thus, the author has not only offered something to be read but has created an object which forces contemplation. A small group of his sonnets will illustrate with economy his procedure:

The Hottentot

Mild, melancholy, and sedate he stands,
Tending another's flocks upon the fields,
His father's once, where now the White Man builds
His home, and issues forth his proud commands:
His dark eye flashes not; his listless hands
Support the Boor's huge firelock—but the shields
And quivers of his race are gone: he yields,
Submissively, his freedom and his lands.
Has he no courage? Once he had—but, lo!
The felon's chain hath worn him to the bone.
No enterprise? Alas! the brand—the blow—
Have humbled him to dust—his Hope is gone!
"He's a base-hearted hound, not worth his food";
His Master cries—"he has no *gratitude*!" [26]

The Bushman

The Bushman sleeps within his black-brow'd den,
In the lone wilderness: around him lie
His wife and little ones unfearingly—
For they are far away from "Christian men."
No herds, loud lowing, call him down the glen;

He fears no foe but famine; and may try
To wear away the hot noon slumberingly;
Then rise to search for roots—and dance again.
But he shall dance no more! His secret lair,
Surrounded, echoes to the thundering gun,
And the wild shriek of anguish and despair!
He dies—yet, ere life's ebbing sands are run,
Leaves to his sons a curse, should they be friends
With the proud Christian race—"for they are fiends!" [27]

THE CAFFER

Lo! where he crouches by the kloof's dark side,
Eyeing the farmer's lowing herds afar;
Impatient watching, till the evening star
Lead forth the twilight dim, that he may glide
Like panther to the prey. With freeborn pride
He scorns the herdsman, nor regards the scar
Of recent wound—but burnishes for war
His assagai and targe of buffalo hide.
He is a robber?—True; it is a strife
Between the black-skinned bandit and the white.
A savage?—Yes; though loth to aim at life,
Evil for evil fierce he doth requite.
A heathen?—teach him, then, thy better creed,
Christian, if thou deserv'st that name indeed! [28]

Regardless of how little South African history, anthropology, or ethnology a reader of these sonnets knows for the three groups depicted here he will understand immediately the great difference in native reaction to the coming of Europeans. Bushmen resisted in every way the white man. Terms offered by the bush people were the same as those of the animals of the veld. Thus, this group was hunted to extinction, or near extinction, along with most of the wild life of the area. Both Bantu and Boer pursued Bushmen in what approached perilously close to being considered a "sport" on one side—bitter tragedy on the other. Thus, these men of the veld finally vanished, except for the few who retreated to the desert lands. Hottentots followed a course which led them into a kind of captivity which became virtual slavery. Without the temperament to resist in the manner of the Bushmen and without the size and strength to fight as the Bantu (Caffers or Kaffirs), they became the victims of Boer movement inland. Those whom Pringle terms "Caffers" were of the great warrior tribes, large and powerful, with no idea of surrender.

In the sonnets it is immediately apparent that with clarity and directness Pringle has identified a major distinguishing characteristic of each native group. Difference in setting is established through specific and appropriate images. The Hottentot appears in the fields, attending the flocks, and "his listless hands/ Support the Boor's huge firelock." "The Bushman sleeps within his black-brow'd den,/ In the lone wilderness," but in the afternoon he will "rise to search for roots—and dance again." The Caffer "crouches by the kloof's dark side," where he "burnishes for war/ His assagai and targe. . . ." In each sonnet, the white man is the opposing force. He enslaves the Hottentot, murders the Bushman, and fails to make a "believer" of the Caffer, whose name meant "unbeliever." The name, of course, was relevant in only one context–an "unbeliever" in relation to those who applied the term to the Bantu peoples. Pringle certainly considered himself a true believer, and it is abundantly clear that he approached the shores of South Africa with missionary intentions, although not professional. It is impossible to read many pages in either his verse or prose without encountering his passionate desire to change heathen beings into Christians. The sonnet on the Bushman is a bitter attack on the absence of Christian action and the lines on the Caffer a challenge to the Christian to convert the heathen. In both, the author is concerned with the discrepancy between theory and practice. In his attitude Pringle was thoroughly normal for the time. Because they would have assumed they were on Pringle's side, many of those actually being condemned in the sonnets would have been much surprised. To be quite accurate, it is necessary to admit that in this particular attitude Pringle himself was not always consistent—in fact, occasionally contradictory. His poems, however, maintain a unified tone and point of view. Few samples from his work illustrate more completely this quality than these sonnets. Evidence of later reaction to the material here being discussed emerges from the fact that in the *New Centenary Book of South African Verse*, 1945, Francis Carey Slater used seven of Pringle's poems, three of them coming from this small collection of sonnets.

How filled with missionary thoughts was the mind of Thomas Pringle may be seen in an examination of the fourteen sonnets appearing in the South African section of his 1828 volume. With "On Visiting a Missionary Settlement," April 1821, he introduces the group.[29] Then, after his consideration of the Hottentot, Bushman, and Caffer, he celebrates the Moravian settlement at Genadendal. From an examination of locations, he turned toward the concept of the work itself in "The Good Missionary," who "left his Christian friends and native strand,/ By pity for benighted men constrain'd."[30] His great aim was "To serve his God, and gather souls to heaven."[31] Thus, six of the fourteen sonnets touch this subject very directly, others impinging upon it in various ways.

Almost inseparable from Pringle's interest in missionary work was his passionate concern for human freedom and his detestation of its opposite—the institution of slavery. One of the bitterest of his sonnets is on "Slavery"[32] and perhaps equally bitter the one "To Oppression."[33] The opposite of these two is the sonnet in which he praises the Huguenots, who had settled in South Africa near the end of the seventeenth century. Today at Franschhoek an impressive monument reminds the world of this tiny minority which had so much influence upon the country. Of them Pringle wrote, "By Faith supported and by Freedom led,/ A fruitful field amidst the desert making,/ They dwelt secure, when kings and priests were quaking,/ And taught the waste to yield them wine and bread."[34] For this sonnet Pringle found that history had created his materials for him, and he was not afraid to use them in their pure state. The Huguenots were a religious group; therefore "Faith" was crucially significant in the moves they made. Since "Freedom" was denied them in France, they were forced to leave home to retain their freedom. In their new location, they literally taught the lands upon which they settled to yield them "wine and bread," food which sustained life but likewise the ingredients of the Holy Communion. It is this section of South Africa that has become one of the great wine producing areas of the world. In a distant land was created a little of France. Before concluding the sonnet sequence in *Ephemerides,* Pringle offered his readers a poem "To the Cape." Perhaps no other lines that he wrote reveal quite so accurately and with such complete directness his attitude toward South Africa. It was at the Cape that he received his first view of the country, and it was also the land that he saw last as his ship moved into the Atlantic on the voyage back to England. The Cape had witnessed his greatest success and likewise his most absolute defeat. With all of this stored in his mind he wrote:

> O Cape of Storms! although thy front be dark,
> And bleak thy naked cliffs and cheerless vales,
> And perilous thy fierce and faithless gales
> To staunchest mariner and stoutest bark;
> And, though along thy coasts with grief I mark
> The servile and the slave,—with him who wails
> An exile's lot,—and blush to hear thy tales
> Of sin and sorrow, and oppression stark:—
> Yet, spite of physical and moral ill,
> And, after all I've seen and suffer'd here,
> There are strong links that bind me to thee still,
> And render even thy rocks and deserts dear:
> Here dwell kind hearts, which time nor place can chill—
> Loved kindred, and congenial friends sincere.[35]

Writing in the 1820's, Thomas Pringle took his position as the first of a succession of authors who built compositions around the almost fantastic visual images which impinged upon the human eye as it approached by sea the Cape of Good Hope. Initially in history, the emotion created was fear because of the "fierce . . . gales," which were not made more cheerful by the "dark . . . bleak . . . naked cliffs. . . ." Sailors encountering seas and shores of this description usually longed for the safety of home. Though in the poem Pringle admits that he "wails/ An exile's lot," he starts what he has to say with an "although" in the first line. Thus, although there is danger, servitude, slavery, sin, sorrow, and oppression, there have been experiences that "render even thy rocks and deserts dear." A few years after the little exiled Scot wrote these lines, there was born in South Africa a baby who was to be the first (as far as is known) native South African poet to long in absence for the fierceness and terror of the Cape. William Rodger Thomson (1832–67), who died even younger than Pringle, lived long enough to write lines his country has remembered.

Its beetling crags rise vast, and war
With oceans, meeting from afar,
To break their billows on its shore
With fearful, never-ending roar.

Bold mariners who sailed of old
Through unknown seas in search of gold,
Saw those dark rocks, those giant forms,
And, fear-quelled, named them "Cape of Storms."
O land of storms, I pine to hear
That music which made others fear;
I long to see thy storm—fiend scowl,
I long to hear the fierce winds howl,
Hot with fell fires across thy plains.

Thou glorious land! where Nature reigns
Supreme in awful loveliness.
O shall thy exiled son not bless
Those hills and dales of thine, where first
He roamed a careless child. . . .

Land of "Good Hope," thy future lies
Bright 'fore my vision as thy skies!
O Africa! long lost in night,
Upon the horizon gleams the light
Of Breaking dawn. . . .[36]

Everything about Thomson's words indicates that he had a real love for his country, and he laments absence from it. More than half a century later, and a hundred years after Pringle, Roy Campbell, in exiling himself from South Africa, used the famous continental extremity as a symbol in "Rounding the Cape."[37] Campbell echoes the ambivalence present in Pringle's poem:

The low sun whitens on the flying squalls,
Against the cliffs the long grey surge is rolled
Where Adamastor from his marble halls
Threatens the sons of Lusus as of old.

Faint on the glare uptowers the dauntless form,
Into whose shade abysmal as we draw,
Down on our decks, from far above the storm,
Grin the stark ridges of his broken jaw. . . .

Farewell, terrific shade! though I go free
Still of the powers of darkness art thou Lord:
I watch the phantom sinking in the sea
Of all that I have hated or adored.[38]

Sequences of this kind—Pringle to Thomson to Campbell—reveal how Thomas Pringle fits into South African poetry in English. Indebtedness is not being suggested. What has happened is probably much more significant than anything which might be demonstrated by playing the game of influences. The fact to note is that from the beginning Pringle was employing some of the materials which not only proved useful to him but would be of value to those who followed. After a century of kneading, these raw materials reached Roy Campbell, William Plomer, and others, the materials now ready for transformation into symbols.

CHAPTER 7

One Endeavor Ends in Victory

LOVE of poetry was the presiding principle of Thomas Pringle's life, and a passion for establishing human independence and living Christianity was the generating force within his being. As was clearly demonstrated by his South African sonnets, the two were inextricably mingled inside his mind and often were manifested externally in his poems. His actions, however, were frequently determined by the need to make a living for himself and his wife. The struggle had started in Edinburgh. Everything within drove him to a life of writing; everything outside him made it quite definite that he had to obtain the necessities which sustain life before he could assure his existence to write. Regardless of how complex his motives may have been for going to South Africa, one which cannot be ignored is that he could no longer be assured of a living in Scotland, at least not the kind that he wanted. In 1822 at the Cape, he himself said, "Had I remained in Edinburgh I might have sunk deeper into difficulties. . . . I came here to mend my fortunes and pay my debts." [1]

Despite all of the other implications of his conflict with the governor in Cape Town, the first result was economic ruin. There would be no chance for him in South Africa until Lord Somerset was gone. All that was left for Thomas was a return, this time to London. Though he did not leave Cape Town without plans and some slight prospects, his employment for the next seven years resulted from his passion for human independence. The Anti-Slavery Society needed a secretary, and Thomas Pringle was seeking employment. In the same place man and moment coincided, and Thomas accepted the position which must have given him more satisfaction than any other undertaking of his life up to that point. Here, finally, he won a victory.

Though it seems rather certain that the ideas of an article published in London late in 1826 guided the Anti-Slavery Society to Pringle, his experiences while at the Cape and his writing skill supplied the organization with what was most urgently needed at this moment in the history of the movement. Initially, it must have been his ability to say "I have seen" or "I have known" that became the basis for ideas expressed in the *New Monthly Magazine* article which won him the secretaryship. Thus, experience linked with the habit of writing constantly and rapidly under pressure made it possible for Thomas to move with ease into his new work.

Despite all of the noble things which can be said about the man and his labor, the first reward must have been the long sought economic security. Despite the fact that the salary was not sufficient to help in paying his debts, it was enough for modest living at the moment. Almost at once after he was settled into his position, Pringle began to look for additional endeavors which would enable him to begin paying what he owed. For this reason he undertook the editorship of *Friendship's Offering*, which he described as one of the several elegant annuals that had become very popular.[2] In 1829 he wrote that the undertaking "is doing well and stands fairly high among the annuals. 7,000 copies are already sold off. . . . When fairly established, it will be worth £150 to £200 to me for many years to come and when one has otherwise but a slender income that is not to be despised." [3] In addition to this kind of work, he did revisions for writers who thought they had something to say but who were unsure of risking publication without professional aid. The fact was that Pringle undertook any honest work which would assist in relieving him of past obligations. Early in 1833 he reported to a friend that he was slowly paying what he owed and hoped that in a few more years he might be cleared of all debt. These few years were not granted him, but he seems to have died almost solvent. The immediate good sale of *A Narrative of a Residence in South Africa* (1834) promised to help in the long economic struggle. Though he was never to see the fulfillment, possibility of success by a serious book must have been profoundly satisfying to him.

Residence in London does not appear to have been good for Pringle physically. Late in 1829 he was seriously ill, and in June he spoke of going to Scotland for his health. A move to Highgate seems to have improved his condition, and he explained that travelling each day into London atop a stagecoach was a great benefit to his health and that their home in Highgate was delightful. To Fairbairn he confided that what he suffered for almost three years before moving from London was indescribable.[4] At the time Highgate was no more than a village separated from London by four miles of open country. Carlyle had made the place and time famous by his comment that during this period the aging Coleridge "sat on the brow of Highgate Hill . . . looking down on London and its smoke-tumult, like a sage escaped from the inanity of life's battle." [5]

One of the rewards of Pringle's work with the society was the chance that it offered of knowing men such as William Wilberforce, Sir Foxwell Buxton, Zachary Macaulay, and Thomas Clarkson. His association with them was close enough to earn at least some invitations to their homes. From the residence of Wilberforce, Highwood Hill, January 23, 1830, Thomas wrote his wife he had discovered he was given the best bedroom. At dinner he not only met the Wilberforce family but a Mr. Simeon from Cambridge, a clergyman, and two ladies. In his letter to Margaret, he remarks that at nine o'clock the company assembled in the hall for family worship and that after the service the group sat around the fireside and talked about poetry and other subjects until after midnight.[6]

Here in this letter to Margaret is another of the many examples of Pringle's continued association with poetry, even in the very midst of his feverish work to bring about abolition of slavery. In 1829, a year after publication of the first collection of his poems containing South African material, he wrote Fairbairn, at the Cape, saying that his African poetry continued to be popular.[7] The claim was not only true but perhaps in one sense an understatement, for all subsequent evidence indicates that it was the South African material—both prose and verse—which developed and preserved the name of Thomas Pringle as an author. The reason for this reaction is very simple. As an English-Scottish writer, Pringle was in competition with Wordsworth, Coleridge, Byron, Shelley, and Keats— to name only a few. Tennyson was already publishing and known to him. Yet when Pringle wrote as a South African, he was alone and from the beginning was able to find an audience ready to listen.

Readers were not only following Thomas Pringle the poet of South Africa; they were following also Pringle the abolitionist.

In considering Pringle in this role, a reader should be very careful to remember all aspects of this very delicate situation. As a child Thomas had exhibited a headstrong desire for independence —first, it must be admitted, for himself—but soon for others. Later, his desperate moves at the Cape to free the press from government control, to secure independence for the journalistic profession, were recorded in detail, both by himself and by others. Very soon after he reached South Africa, he commenced his study of conditions among the native population. It is important to remember that Pringle had a far more intimate knowledge of native conditions than most of the men with whom he was associated in the abolition movement. Despite all of the passion with which he advocated reform, he never displayed the fanaticism of some of his fellow workers. It was this lack of information on the part of the theorists, often residing at a distance, which disturbed men living with the actual problem. Thomas Pringle had, for a part of his mature years, lived in the very midst of the complex situation. Before darkness fell on his first night at Baviaans River, he had to set a watch against surprise attack. In his little book on the conditions under which the 1820 Settlers lived, he made proposals concerning defense. When he returned to the frontier in 1825, he was almost immediately reminded of the native attacks and exploded against the Bushmen. He called them "ungrateful *schelms!* even after I have celebrated them in song." [8] Of Pringle at this moment a twentieth-century biographer has remarked that when he himself became personally involved his sentimentality was replaced by anger. Thomas wrote Fairbairn that he had ordered a commando against them. "You see," he explained, "we back-settlers grow all savage & bloody by coming in continual collision with savages." [9] Fairbairn, safe in Cape Town, upbraided him for his conduct, and Thomas replied, "Your damnations against my Bushmen Commandoes do not alarm me. There is no 'damned spot' on my hands. But I am no quaker to turn my cheek to the [? Monster]–& if attacked will resist even to slaying [? him then, approve] who he may." [10]

Evidence of this kind suggests that attitudes toward the natives were determined by the distance of the reactor from the object motivating the reaction. This conclusion, however, is not accurate because it is merely partial. Among the few absolute judgments which can be proposed in considering this whole question is to say that those who are certain they know all of the answers are wrong and those who assume the problem is simple are wrong. Usually these two groupings merge into one because certainty that solutions are easy and near develops from the belief that the problems being encountered are definite and simple. Regardless of how completely Thomas Pringle agreed with the aims of men of this kind (and he did agree with them, passionately), he had experienced enough to save him from some of their harshness. Moving rapidly toward what was to be the work of his last years and acting as if consciously preparing himself for his place in the Anti-Slavery Society, in June, 1825, Pringle made an extended visit to the home of Captain Sir Andries Stockenstrom. Upon this trip he was in the company of Dr. John Philip, now on a tour of the missions under his direction, and James Read, also associated with the missionary efforts in South Africa. While there, they were also joined by the Reverend William Wright, who was returning from a journey through Kaffirland missions. Captain Stockenstrom, landdrost of Graaff-Reinet, is a useful person to examine in a study of the native situation of South Africa. His father had been killed near the Zureberg by a party of Kaffirs. Despite the loss, this man was able to bring to the native problem a balanced point of view. Of these visitors in his home during the month of June, 1825, he recorded in his autobiography the following comment:

It is well known that these gentlemen were at the time not only in opposition to, but in direct collision with the local Government, and it was by some people deemed at least strange that such "radicals" should be the guests of the chief magistrate of the district. However, I was master in my own house; there was no hotel in the place in those days, and I found these gentlemen very agreeable society. There were some warm debates on all the topics then exciting the public mind. The liberty of the press was of course paramount. On this point, as on many other matters calling for revision, improvement, or reform, we were pretty well agreed. The aborigines came, you may be sure, next to, if not before the press.

. . . Wright, having for some time been travelling on the Frontier and through Kaffirland, was literally frantic about the injustice and oppression which he had heard of and witnessed and he was enthusiastically backed by his fellow travellers.

> To have denied the extermination of the Hottentots and Bushmen, the possession of their country by ourselves, the cruelties with which their expulsion and just resistance have been accompanied, the hardships with which the laws were still pressing upon their remnants, the continuation of the same system against the Kaffirs, and the iniquity of the aggressors and murders then lately perpetrated upon the latter race, would have been ridiculous as well as dishonest, as there was not in the Colony, even among the Boors, one single being of the slightest decency or respectability who did not see the facts before his eyes and lament them. I should by such denial have given the lie to much that I had myself complained of and for years been trying to mitigate or resist.[11]

With the exception of Thomas, the visitors, who were uninvolved in daily practical aspects of the native world, became quite fanatical. Of them Stockenstrom said that they "tried my temper by the virulence with which they persisted in denouncing the present generation of the colonists and refused to make any allowance for their actual position, which rendered self-defence absolutely necessary for the preservation of both parties." [12] Before this important visit to Stockenstrom's home, Pringle had learned enough about the landdrost in matters both related and unrelated to the topics discussed at Graaff-Reinet in 1825 to develop great respect for the man. This attitude now became valuable.

Regardless of how deeply disturbed he was by the obvious extermination of the Bushmen and extreme pressures of various kinds exerted upon the Hottentots, Pringle understood and admitted some of the problems to be encountered in achieving the ends for which he most fervently wished. He knew, for example, that time, perhaps considerable time, was needed to effect the changes desired. Remembering what he had seen around him in many areas of the Cape, he wrote: "Civilisation and information must of necessity make but slow and feeble advances among a class of people so situated as the white back-settlers of the wild and thinly peopled regions on the Bushman frontier. Nor is it the knowledge simply of what is just and right that will induce men to act justly, or wisely, or humanely. Look at the long and arduous struggles we have had in enlightened, humane, and religious England to obtain the abolition of the abominable Slave Trade, and of the not less abominable State of Slavery. Look at the depth of ungenerous and unchristian prejudice in regard to the coloured race, which pervades free and religious America, like a feculent moral fog. I do not consider the Dutch-African colonists as worse than other people would be and have been in similar circumstances—not certainly worse than the Spaniards in America—not worse perhaps than the British in Australia." [13] Here is being exhibited a charity which most, or many, of his associates withheld. Thus, though he often grieved for the condition of the dark inhabitants of South Africa, he did not forget that there was another group to be considered. With his own experiences in mind, he commented, "Moreover, having been myself for years resident on a frontier exposed to the incursions of the native tribes, and witness to the annoyance and damage sustained by my own relatives from the depredations, it can scarcely be supposed that I am insensible to the provocations often received by the colonists, or altogether without sympathy for *their* situation. But on that very account I am more deeply impressed with the conviction of their unfitness to be the judges or the avengers of their own wrongs. Were they the most humane and enlightened people in the world, they could not safely be trusted with such perilous powers. Without strong *legal restraints,* such, alas! is human nature on the large scale, that mere humanity will always be too feeble for passion and selfishness." [14]

Though Pringle's position, which made his name known to thousands around the world, and his writing for the society often brought upon him attacks from many directions, securing even the slightest perspective served to differentiate Pringle from such men as Dr. Philip. It has been suggested that Dr. Philip's *Researches in South Africa,* 1828, created more controversy and bad feeling in the country than anything published up to that time. While it was indeed impossible to refute much of what he said and though conditions at the time were in many ways deplorable, men such as Sir Andries Stockenstrom accused Dr. Philip of untruthfulness at times and upon other occasions of gross exaggeration.[15] Pringle, now far from the provocations and exasperations of the frontier, naturally supported Dr. Philip, for the "cause" had become his very life. Yet most of the statements given in this chapter have been taken from Pringle's *Narrative,* put into its final form near the end of his life and published just before death in 1834. Preparation of the book for the press was being done after seven years of intensive work for the Anti-Slavery Society and at that time when he was farthest from his experiences at the Cape. These passages represent his final comments on the subject.

Months and years of hard work by the committee—and certainly this means the secretary, also—had its effect. In general, the cause was approved by the London press. Communications to Pringle demonstrated that the movement was being backed by an increasing number of men. Women gave wide support to the gathering force, and letters from distant places showed that the world was watching what was happening in London.

Finally, political success was achieved. On August 28, 1833, an act of Parliament abolished slavery. Manumission came a year later. A document presenting the Act of Abolition, signed by Thomas Pringle, was published June 27, 1834. On August 1, 1834, slavery was formally ended. For most of the men involved in this movement, the cause had exacted a total life of devotion. The whole political career of William Wilberforce had been given to this effort, and the day after Parliament passed the Act of Abolition he died, knowing his work was completed. In November 1833 Pringle wrote Fairbairn, "the great work is *done*. And now, the work accomplished heaven is taking the workmen fast from among us. Wilberforce is departed. Clarkson is both blind & lame, & cannot hold out long. Macaulay is busting [or breaking] up fast; & what Buxton said to me some years [ago] may probably soon be realised. I was expressing apprehensions about Macaulay's health: 'He's beginning to get feeble,' said Buxton: but Macaulay will live till Slavery is abolished, & then he will go out like the snuff of a taper'; and it looks like it." [16] All of this was foreshadowing. The day after he signed the paper announcing the formal abolition of slavery, Thomas Pringle gave the first signs of the disease which in four months would carry him to the grave.

CHAPTER 8

The Great Narrative Is Published

SINCE the May morning in 1820 when Thomas Pringle sat upon the deck of the *Brilliant* and recorded what was passing before him as the ship tacked along the South African coast, he had been preparing the book which in 1834 was finished, at least as far as time and conditions made completion possible. In May of what was to be his last year of life, he sent John Fairbairn a copy of the *Narrative of a Residence in South Africa* and commented, "You will find that I have *spoken out*. Whether it will please M. Stanley & some of our autocratic Whigs I know not, but I was determined that, happen to myself what may, they should have the truth (or rather such a portion as I could put into my book) for once. Perhaps you will not thank me for saying what I thought of you. I am sure you will suffer for it by the excited rage of the *vermin* around you, who will no doubt pour forth their privy malice on you along with myself & the Dr. [Dr. John Philip] in consequence of what I have said of them. But what signifies *their* enmity. They cannot harm you, I think, more than they have done already—& *our-names*, & what is better our *deeds* will survive when they & all that belongs to them will be swept into the gulf of oblivion." [1]

Turning immediately from a concern for reputation, present and future, he explained something of the practical details of publication. "The prose portion of my book does not contain half the matter I could have put into it—but I thought it would be rash to extend it to two volumes . . . it will require a sale of 800 copies to clear my expenses merely, so that even if I sell off my edition of 1,000 copies I will hardly have any profit. However if it serve (as I trust it will) the higher purpose I had in view, I care little about the profits—poor as I still am. You & I have been wonderfully provided for. . . . So you see things are coming round at last to a right state—& you and I (obscure lads as we were once) are now of some little weight in the world. And yet, if we have any merit, it is chiefly under God's merciful guidance that we have been always *honest men*, & consequently sound & consistent in our views & course of action."[2]

Though he needed every shilling which might accrue to him from the sale of his book, he moved with obvious ease in his comments from profit to achievement. As yet he had received no warning that death was near, but unknowing he made the proper choice. Leaving books for the future was now far more important than all the pounds sterling in the exchequer. With these pages of prose, he began to establish the place in the world for which he had longed. His duties as secretary of the Anti-Slavery Society had made his name known, although at times it was viewed with anathema; but now that he had something to sell, he could use the fact that at least he was known; and, after all, the movement he had fervently supported had received the approval of many thousands. That there did exist a concern for the ideas he expressed is evidenced by the publication within a year, 1835, of a new edition, this with a biographical sketch of the author. Other editions came quickly. Almost immediately after its initial appearance in 1834, the text was translated into German, and thus the book received European presentation as early as 1836. Clearly, Thomas Pringle had given the world something in which it was interested.

I *The Kind of Book that Pringle Wrote*

Perhaps it is not unfair to suggest that Pringle's established practice of lifting materials from his journal and lack of time for the writing of a new thoroughly organized study of his years in the Cape determined the nature of the book he called *Narrative of a Residence in South Africa*. The volume finally published in 1834 had been announced in a prospectus dated from Cape Town, January 1, 1825. Since actual printing seems to have been intended before the end of 1825 or early 1826, it is necessary to assume that much of the material to be used was drawn directly from the journal. In 1824 Pringle had worked in this way because of an immediate need of articles for his magazine. At this same time he turned to information gathered earlier when haste was required in preparing *Some Account of the Present State of the English Settlers in Albany, South Africa*. Much of what went into the *Narrative of a Residence* must have been held in abeyance after his return from South Africa until Parliament passed the act which abolished slavery. In less than a year following Parliament's decision, he had his book in print, and before the end of the year (and his life) he had made the preparations for the second edition.

Despite the very loose organization of the *Narrative,* it probably achieved more success than any rigidly planned text might have developed. As published, the book offered not one type of material but several. Seemingly the original intention was to write a narrative. For readers back in Europe, the story of a trip to South Africa would be an exciting adventure, and the normal curiosity of readers was amply satisfied with this aspect of Pringle's work. Closely related to the narrative parts of the book are the sections presenting the animals and birds of the area. Into some of these sections being written to give information, the author reverses his process and inserts brief stories, such as his lion stories. Here, then, complete, was one kind of book.

Travels about the Cape became the second book Pringle was engaged in writing. Movements about the country could have been absorbed with ease into the narrative portions of the text, but Pringle's journeys were serious investigations into the nature of the inhabitants and the country which he was beginning to accept as his own. What he sought was not only for personal use but for publication, and he wished not only to inform his readers but to direct their thinking. This explains why an examination of the mission stations within the Cape was to become the basis for an important part of his book. His visits to missionary establishments turned his mind more and more to the part being taken by the church in the development of South Africa.

Finally, and as published quite separate from the remainder of the volume, Pringle devoted several long chapters to the native inhabitants of South Africa—Bushmen, Hottentots, and Kaffirs. Though he wrote as a laymen for the general reader, there is present some suggestion of a systematic approach to his subject. Most of the studies by scientists were still in the future, but Pringle was at least making a start.

II *The Author as a Storyteller*

Available evidence does not suggest that Thomas Pringle thought of himself as a teller of stories, yet his ability in this direction was very considerable. In fact, a reader is led to speculate upon what he would have written if he had lived in another time or if he had seriously considered developing the talents he had as a narrator. Since neither of these suggestions can ever become a reality, a student of the *Narrative* is tempted to eliminate all elements except the story and then examine the characteristics of what is left. If this were done, a reader would find himself with a skillfully organized series of happenings moving rapidly to periodic climaxes.

Though using actual events as raw material and thus being unable to determine in many ways the course of his narrative, he has by selection and effective presentation created a story in which a reader will find himself immediately interested. Regardless of how profoundly concerned the author was with his decision to abandon home, friends, country and to sail thousands of miles to begin life in an undeveloped area of the world, as narrator he put all of this aside in one paragraph. His second paragraph places the reader beside him as the ship sails to its anchorage in Simon's Bay and every eye strains to see details along a coast being erased by night slipping across the land from the sea. In their eagerness to behold something of Africa, a few of the passengers remained on watch throughout the night. Even those who had gone off to bed were up at dawn to get the first possible glimpse of their new country. At that moment Pringle introduces his reader to the Cape through a verbal exclamation by one of the Scottish party.

Since the emigrants are not to live in Cape Town and only Thomas is allowed to land there while the ship receives provisions, the author soon hurries on up the Indian Ocean coast in the direction of Algoa Bay. As the ship approaches the territory toward which the settlers are moving, Pringle begins to describe the shore along which they are passing. Slipped into the setting being created by the images presented and the action emerging from the voyage is the reaction of a central human intelligence strategically placed.

. . . As we passed headland after headland, the sylvan recesses of the bays and mountains opened successively to our gaze, like a magnificent panorama, continually unfolding new features, or exhibiting new combinations of scenery, in which the soft and the stupendous, the monotonous and the picturesque, were strangely blended. The aspect of the whole was impressive, but sombre; beautiful, but somewhat savage. There was the grandeur and the grace of nature, majestic and untamed; and there was likewise that air of *lonesomeness* and dreary *wildness,* which a country unmarked by the traces of human industry or of human residence seldom fails to exhibit to the view of civilised man. Seated on the poop of the vessel, I gazed alternately on that solitary shore, and on the bands of emigrants who now crowded the deck or leaned along the gangway; some silently musing, like myself, on the scene before us; others conversing in separate groups, and pointing with eager gestures to the country they had come so far to inhabit. Sick of the wearisome monotony of a long sea voyage . . . all were highly exhilarated by the prospect of speedily disembarking; but the sublimely stern aspect of the country, so different from the rich tameness of ordinary English scenery, seemed to strike many of the *Southron* [English as opposed to Scots] with a degree of awe approaching to consternation. The Scotch, on the contrary, as the stirring recollections of their native land were vividly called up by the rugged peaks and shaggy declivities of this wild coast, were strongly affected, like all true mountaineers on such occasions. Some were excited to extravagant spirits; others silently shed tears.[3]

Here Pringle is using a technique of the fictionist, as he alternates between the external and the internal—between the environment through which his characters move and their human reaction to it. In fact, a careful examination of the passage will show that the author is not merely using the methods of the fictionist but has become a fictionist. There was no way for him to determine with any completeness what more than a hundred people were thinking. Though his statements may be quite accurate, he himself has created them.

Now, as does any novelist or short story writer, he turns from mental to physical action. The ship sails into harbor, and again description dominates the page—for this is the land they are to possess. Upon this fact there is a paragraph of meditation.

It being too late to get ashore that evening, we continued gazing on this scene till long after sunset,—till twilight had darkened into night, and the constellations of the southern hemisphere, revolving in cloudless brilliancy above, reminded us that nearly half the globe's expanse intervened between us and our native land—the homes of our youth, and the friends we had parted from for ever; and that here, in this farthest nook of Southern Africa, we were now about to receive the portion of our inheritance, and to draw an irrevocable lot for ourselves and for our children's children. Solemn reflections will press themselves at such a time on the most thoughtless; and this night, as we swung at anchor in Algoa Bay, so long the bourne of all our wishes, many a wakeful brain among us was doubtless expatiating, each according to the prevailing current of thought, in serious meditation on the future or the past. A long sea voyage, and, far more, one with such an object as we had before us, totally disconnecting us for a time from the bustling world behind and before, and from the great political and social interests of humanity, appears, as it were, like a pause or interlude between the acts of the busy drama of human life, and deepens the interest both of the past and the future, by affording a convenient space for reflection. This quiet interval was about to close with us; and we now waited with anxiety for the curtain to draw up, and unfold, in all the distinctness of reality, the scenes of novelty and adventure to which we had so long looked forward.[4]

Action now fills the pages. Early the following morning Pringle goes ashore, finds the proper official, and secures permission for his party to land. Just as the Scottish party reaches land after months at sea, he is informed that an error has been made and they must again board the ship to await their turn. The party faces once more the sea, but Thomas rides off into the interior in search of a mission station located in the vicinity. Finally the Pringles do land and start toward their location, with the excitement which comes from exploring a strange and certainly for them unusual country. Hour by hour the scene changes. The passage inland becomes more and more difficult. At last, with great effort, they break through one final physical barrier and gaze across their own valley, several thousand feet above the sea and surrounded by snow-powdered mountains. This is the first great climax.

In a well-plotted story, one thing ends by establishing the beginning of another. Reaching their destination meant the beginning of the work to create a new home. Action followed upon action in a succession of busy days and months. Some of the things which happened were expected but others unexpected. A few events which were anticipated did not happen at all. Thus the narrative is not without suspense.

Cumulatively, the story moves toward success, and the next major climax. At the end of the second year, it was definite that the Pringle party had reached some understanding of the situation and had secured a firm grip on their grant of land, and the last of the Pringle brothers arrived from Scotland with his family. The allotment on which Thomas was living was being held for this brother. Simultaneously with his arrival, Thomas received an appointment to the newly created South African Library of Cape Town. Again, as one series of events ended, another commenced. Thomas now set out for Cape Town, where events previously not even a part of his nightmares were to rush upon him.

At first there was no indication of the course that events were to take. Thomas was given a period of calm in which he assumed his duties at the library, accepted a few students for instruction because of the need to increase his income, and began to make plans for the publication of a magazine at the Cape.

Days, which at first proceeded in an orderly fashion, became disorderly. Tensions, and finally open conflict, developed, which could end only with the destruction of one side or the other. A climax was reached, and Pringle was driven from Cape Town and finally from South Africa.

Now in London, the chief character of the story continues life in a new environment and with employment of a type not previously attempted. Yet here again there is a specific goal toward which he is working. This time his efforts are leading to success. Here the story is moving towards a climax. Many a novelist has depended upon a less satisfactory plot. Though history gave Thomas Pringle much of his story, he must be given credit for the judiciousness with which he selected what was to be used and for the skill with which individual events were presented.

III *Altar and Hearth*

Because Thomas Pringle regularly availed himself of every opportunity to visit South African missions and homes, his book furnishes enough material for a revealing study of these areas of life in the Cape at this time. He started his investigations just at sunset his first day ashore. Approaching the mission as the flocks and herds were driven in for the night, he was nostalgically reminded of the glens of Scotland. The first close look, however, dispelled all thoughts of home, for both animals and herdsmen told him he was in Africa. Within a few minutes after arrival, he was received by the missionary in charge and witnessed his first example of the handling by government of the native situation. Here was the beginning of what was to become his preparation for that which gave him the right to speak concerning conditions in South Africa.

Some balance for this experience at the mission was achieved even before the Pringle party reached its location. The event at Bethelsdorp had been deeply disturbing to Pringle, but now he was favorably impressed as the group stopped briefly at the home of William Prislo, "Groot William," who was to be a near neighbor. In friendliness the giant Boer welcomed the Scottish party and presented them with vegetables, lemons, and pomegranates. Groot William was not an exception among the Boer residents of the country, for again and again Thomas was to find this friendliness and hospitality as he moved through the Cape.

Though Pringle was ultimately concerned with the human conduct encountered in South Africa, he seems never to have remained unmindful of physical arrangements. Individually his recording of factual details is exact and complete; collectively his pages record much about the area he covered. When he visited the mission at Enon, he noted carefully the order in all the Moravians did. A long paragraph details the hours and activities of their day; then he offers a paragraph in which he demonstrated how this love for order guided them in the laying out of a cemetery:

> Though the Moravians find it impracticable or inexpedient to follow up in their missionary settlements some of the peculiar and rather monastic regulations, which are observed in their European establishments,—such as separating the married and the unmarried, the youth of different sexes, &c., still their precision and formality in classification are very remarkable. Among other peculiarities of this description, I may refer to the singular arrangement of their burial-grounds, which are divided and sub-divided, by walks crossing at right angles, into several compartments. One of these plots, thus marked off, is appropriated for the sepulture of the married missionary brethren and

sisters; a second for the unmarried brothers; a third for the unmarried sisters; a fourth and fifth for baptized and married natives, male and female; a sixth and seventh for the unmarried and unbaptized natives, and so on. This certainly is carrying classification to a most fanciful pitch—especially that of mere mortal dust and ashes! Passing over this, however, there is unquestionably something very touching, as well as tasteful and picturesque, in the appearance of a Moravian burial-ground in South Africa. Situated at some little distance from the village, yet not far from the house of worship, cut out in the centre of a grove of evergreens, and kept as neat as a pleasure garden, the burial-ground of Enon formed a pleasing contrast to the solitary graves, heaped with a few loose stones, or the neglected and dilapidated churchyards, usually met with in the colony. The funeral service, too, of the Moravians is very solemn and impressive. And still more solemn must be the yearly celebration of their service on Easter morn, when the whole population of the settlement is congregated in the burial-ground, to listen to an appropriate discourse from the most venerable of their pastors, accompanied by an affecting commemoration of such of their friends and relatives as may have died within the year, and followed by hymns and anthems, sung by their united voices amidst the ashes of their kindred.[5]

When Pringle made his first overnight visit to a Boer farmer's home, he recorded with precision how the building was constructed:

. . . . The walls were thick, and substantially built of strong adhesive clay; a material, which being well prepared or *tempered,* in the manner of mortar for brick-making, and raised in successive layers, soon acquires, in this dry climate, a great degree of hardness, and is considered scarcely inferior in durability to burnt brick. These walls, which were about nine feet high, and tolerably smooth and straight, had been plastered over within and without with a composition of sand and cowdung, and this being afterwards well white-washed with a sort of pipe-clay, or with lime made of burnt shells, the whole had a very clean and light appearance.

The roof was neatly thatched with a species of hard rushes, which are considered much more durable and less apt to catch fire than straw. . . .

The house was divided into three apartments; the one in which we were seated (called the *voorhuis*) opened immediately from the open air, and is the apartment in which the family always sit, eat, and receive visitors. A private room (*slaap-kamer*) was formed at either end of this hall, by cross partitions of the same height and construction as the outer walls. The floor, which, though only of clay, appeared uncommonly smooth and hard, I found, on inquiry, had been formed of ant-heaps, which, being pounded into dust, and then watered and well stampted, assume a consistency of great tenacity. . . .

The house was lighted by four square windows in front,—one in each of the bed-rooms, and two in the *voorhuis,*—and also by the door, which appeared to be shut only during the night. The door consisted of reeds, rudely fastened on a wicker frame, and was fixed to the door-posts by thongs of bullocks' hide. The windows were without glass, and were closed at night, each with an untanned quagga skin. There was neither stove nor chimney in any part of the dwelling-house; but the operations of cooking were performed in a small circular hut of clay and reeds, which stood in front of it. . . . The bedrooms . . . were furnished each with one or more large bed-steads, or stretchers, without posts or curtains, but provided with good feather-beds, spread on elastic frames, woven with thongs of bullock's hide, like a cane-bottomed chair.[6]

Though Thomas Pringle never intended his factual passages to be used as a practical guide to construction, they might easily be employed as a manual of instruction. What it originally did, and still does, was give his reader a feeling for the existence of these phases of the country about which he writes.

IV *Native Peoples*

Though for a number of years the first twelve chapters of the *Narrative* certainly were close to a condition in which they could be sent to a printer, the last three chapters appear to have been written very near the date of publication. A parenthetical statement a few pages before the end of Chapter 14 says "(April 15, 1834, when I wrote this chapter)."[7] Three pages later, in a note, he says "A file of the South African Advertiser, up to March 1, 1834, (which has just reached me as I am sending these, the last sheets of my volume, to press). . . ."[8] Pringle must have written this note in May, and he sent Fairbairn a copy of the book during the same month. If all of this information is accurate, the printer certainly had everything in type except these last pages and perhaps had printed and gathered all save the final signature, or very near the final one. Regardless of the exact schedule being followed, it was the chapters which discussed the native peoples that claimed Pringle's attention in 1834.

Glancing through materials for a preliminary appraisal, a reader notes—with some surprise—that the author has devoted eight times the number of pages to the Bantu population as to the Bushmen, and between four and five times as much to the Hottentots. The great difference suggests two important facts. First, Pringle knew very little about the Bushmen; second, they were not a crucial practical problem because rapidly becoming extinct. For this reason there was nothing here upon which to launch a crusade. Thus, the Bushmen were rather rapidly dismissed. As between the remaining groups, Pringle was far more deeply involved in an emotional sense with the Hottentots because of his numerous personal experiences. Then, too, in general the Hottentots represented the weak and helpless. To Thomas Pringle there was something immediately appealing about defending these people who could not defend themselves. Conversely, Pringle really did not know the Bantu tribes. The Bantu, however, were numerous, strong, and often could defend themselves. In fact it was obvious they intended to do just that. They became important because they were dangerous. Their numbers, of course, made them attractive since they offered millions of souls to be saved.

Simple lack of information and a desire to prove a particular point guided Pringle in his discussion of the Bushmen. His first claim is that the Bushmen "appear to be the remains of Hottentot hordes, originally subsisting, like all the aboriginal tribes of Southern Africa, chiefly by rearing sheep and cattle. . . ." [9] Continuing, Pringle emphasizes the deterioration of this native group. "Having descended from the pastoral to the hunter state, the Bushmen have, with the increased perils and privations of that mode of life, necessarily acquired a more ferocious and resolute character. From a mild, confiding, and unenterprising race of shepherds, they have been gradually transformed into wandering hordes of fierce, suspicious, and vindictive savages. . . ." [10] In his next paragraph, he charges that European settlers created the fate of the Bush people. "Whether any considerable hordes of these people existed in their present state previous to the occupation of the country by Europeans, seems to be doubtful; but it is certain that numerous tribes, once subsisting in ease and affluence on the produce of their herds and flocks, have by the incessant incroachments of the colonists been either driven to the sterile deserts, and of necessity transformed to Bushmen, or utterly extirpated. This process has been carrying on, as the authentic records of the Colony prove, for at least a hundred and twenty years. And thus on the outskirts of our ever-advancing frontier, numerous wandering hordes of destitute and desperate savages—the South-African 'Children of the Mist'—have been constantly found in a state of precarious truce, or of bitter hostility, with the colonists." [11] Except for a quoted story about the treatment of Bushmen, the author uses only five pages for his discussion.

To make clear what Pringle knew about these early people, one has only to place beside his comments parallel statements from a modern ethnologist:

> In their occupation of South Africa they seem to have extended over almost the whole region from the Zambesi in the north down to the south coast. . . . Even well within historical times Bushmen were living in districts from which they have now completely disappeared, or where perhaps only a few individuals still survive. . . .
>
> But the encroachment of later invading peoples gradually ousted them from the more favorable districts which they occupied. First the Hottentots, advancing south along the west coast, drove them from the fertile plains to the mountain fastnesses of the interior. Then the Bantu, pressing down the east coast, overcame the fierce resistance of the little people upon whose ancient hunting grounds they trespassed. Other Bantu tribes, traversing the interior of the country, came into conflict with the Bushmen in the arid plains north and south of the Orange River and the Vaal and in the rugged mountains to the east. The European settler, in his turn pushing north and east and seeking fresh pastures for his growing herds, waged an equally relentless war against them. . . .[12]

Even a cursory examination of Pringle's comments in relation to the parallel statements written a century later will make clear that the early writer along with his generation generally, was without information made available by extensive research. Some of the findings of this type were already in print, but Pringle's reading was focused upon those who devoted themselves to a particular point of view, not investigations of a total situation using a scientific attitude. Thus, a comparison of the material quoted suggests that Pringle did not know the Bushmen were the oldest of all native peoples of South Africa, with which he was familiar, nor does he seem to realize the extent of their territory. Nothing he says suggests he was aware of migratory periods of Hottentot and Bantu history and of how this affected Bushman existence. His claim that they had "descended from the pastoral to the hunter state" and that they were originally "a mild, confiding . . . race of shepherds . . ." is the opposite of the suggestion that Bantu warriors encountered "the fierce resistance of the little people upon whose ancient hunting grounds they trespassed." In the absence of other evidence, it would be possible to assume from this statement that the Bushmen were hunters but also could be pastoralist. Several pages later, however, the author says, "While the Bushmen are hunters and collectors only, the Hottentots in addition are a pastoral people, with herds of long-horned straight-backed cattle and flocks of fat-tailed hairy sheep." [13] Pringle missed the directional movement of the group with which he was concerned. Instead of Bushmen being degenerate Hottentots, the evidence suggests that Hottentots acquired new blood and characteristics which dissociated them from the Bushmen groups. The following paragraph offers a summary of the theory:

The most plausible theory of the racial origin of the Hottentots may therefore be that they have sprung out of a mixture of the old Bushman population of East Africa with an early immigration there of Hamites, who gave them their cattle and those peculiarities of language by which they are distinguished from the modern Bushman. So far as the slight indications of their legendary history go, they seem to have come originally from somewhere in the region of North-West Tanganyika, and to have wandered with their cattle and sheep between Lakes Tanganyika and Nyasa, and then, perhaps as the result of pressure from behind, across the high plateau of Central Africa, with their faces always towards the setting sun, until they came upon the "great waters" (i.e. the Atlantic), when they turned south, crossing the Kunene, and moved slowly onwards down the west coast of the continent. How long they had been in possession of the coast regions in the south-west of Cape Colony before the Portuguese first saw them in the neighbourhood of Saldanha Bay and later on at Mossel Bay, at the end of the fifteenth century, we have no means of knowing. The few facts that lead us to judge that they had not been in the south for many centuries are based on our knowledge of their movements on the eastern frontier, where in the early eighteenth century their advance guard, formed by a tribe known as the Gonaqua, came into contact with the Bantu peoples, who by that time were slowly pushing westwards along the southern coast of South Africa.[14]

How little Pringle understood of the slowness with which civilizations move and change is evident in his assumption that what had occurred could have taken place within the period of extensive occupation of the Cape by Europeans. Writing deep into the nineteenth century, he speaks of the process being at least a hundred and twenty years in duration—which is already into the eighteenth century. Historical records locate Hottentots at the bottom of the Cape in the fifteenth century, and the suggestion is made that the few facts available indicate that they had not been there *many centuries.* Obviously Hottentot movements have displaced Bushmen much too early for Europeans to do very much after their arrival.

Showing Pringle's errors is not intended to discredit him, but only to demonstrate the weakness of his methods when handling this particular type of material. Again and again, in other parts of the *Narrative* he has proved to be an accurate guide. Even in considering the native question, he often has been a worthy teacher and there will be future occasions to commend his rightness and strength. Merely to establish a few weaknesses in a man is no more than to establish his humanity.

When Pringle turned from consideration of Bushmen to Hottentots, he was able to write on the basis of personal experience. It will be remembered that a Hottentot boy guided him as he sought Bethelsdorp his first day ashore at Algoa Bay. At the mission he saw and heard, for the first time, many Hottentots. Hottentots were the drivers of the oxen that carried the Pringles and their possessions inland. Hottentots were sent to guard the Scottish party in their new location. Their first servants were Hottentots. The enumeration could continue, but here is more than enough to establish Pringle's familiarity with these particular natives.

Starting his chapter on the Hottentots, Pringle says nothing about their origin but goes immediately to the mid-seventeenth century when the Dutch encountered the native inhabitants throughout the country beyond Cape Town. In the beginning there was peace because the Europeans were few in number and required very little land. When the Dutch reached out to acquire significant territorial areas which the Hottentots considered their own, the native answer was *war.* The little brown herdsmen lost the war and accepted a treaty which ceded territory and regulated affairs for some years. With exceptions the period extends up to the eighteenth century. At this point, Pringle's real interest begins and with it his consideration of the fate of the Hottentot people. His concern is with the driving of Hottentots from their lands and then with the destruction of their freedom as human beings. At first, the natives were safe because no precious metals were found nor were the products eagerly sought by Europe produced on the land. The situation changed when settlers discovered that in addition to certain grains the area would support almost unlimited flocks and herds. Unrestrained by any established government, individuals began to move north and east and to appropriate land by force. Next they made raids far inland to capture sheep and cattle. Bereft of land, herds and flocks, all but life, the Hottentots had to work for the Dutch—or perish. The problem for them was that they were offering themselves in a noncompetitive labor market. As more and more Europeans came, the situation of the Hottentots because of their numbers, became worse and worse. Finally their state deteriorated to a point at which Pringle insisted the condition in which they lived was worse than that of the slaves. A slave was property and if destroyed was a loss to the owner. A Hottentot was "free" and if destroyed would merely be replaced by another. Given these details, the results were inevitable. As a distinct ethnic group, the Hottentots were moving towards extinction. Prolonged brutal treatment had certainly affected the spirit of the race. There were exceptions, but the hopelessness of the situation must have guided the reaction of those who survived.

When the English took control of South Africa early in the nineteenth century, they inherited the situation here presented by Pringle. The author offers this as the basis for what he wishes to say about the Hottentots. He himself arrived in the Cape during the period of adjustment. To reverse through the normal processes of government the course of history, especially since final authority remained in London, took time, under the very best of conditions; meanwhile much could be done by individuals and smaller groups to start the process. Here was an almost perfect situation for the employment of Pringle's talents as a writer, and he certainly used his ability upon every possible occasion.

Early in this account, Pringle filled four pages in relating "the extinction of the last independent kraal, or horde, of free Hottentots within the colony."[15] Building his account around the life and fate of the Stuurman brothers, the author offers what might have been a summary for a historical novel of the period. The movement of the story is already definite, and the author is beginning to shape his characters. Though there is no intention of implying that Pringle contemplated writing a novel, there is every reason to suggest that his narrative instinct was often called into use and employed to stir the reader's emotions.

After relating the life of the Stuurmans, events which occurred a decade before his arrival at the Cape, Pringle commenced a consideration of the life of Hottentots while he was a resident. Because conditions were in many instances determined by their legal status, Pringle shifted from South Africa to England for an exposition of what was being done by the government in London to relieve this part of the South African population, which though not in a state of legal slavery was not actually free. He was familiar with all of the legal details because he was now in England. Immediately upon the settlement in Parliament of the legal question, Pringle turned the reader's attention back to South Africa to present the effect upon the people of the country. What he expected to hear may be predicted easily and likewise what he hoped to prove on the basis of action in comparison with popular predictions. First, he explained what the country said would happen when the Hottentots were given freedom: "The absolute ruin of the colony from this measure was loudly and confidently predicted. It was asserted that the fields would lie untilled, and the flocks go untended, for want of labourers and herdsmen; and that the white inhabitants generally would be reduced to ruin from this cause, and by being plundered by marauding hordes of Hottentot banditti. For it was assumed, as a result not to be questioned, that no Hottentot would work unless compelled by coercion, and that the whole race would betake themselves to a life of idleness, vagrancy, and robbery, when no longer held in servitude by compulsory laws. . . ."[16] What actually happened he presented in considerable detail, the summary passages of which are here quoted:

> . . . immediately on the promulgation of the Ordinance, vagrancy to a considerable extent did take place among the Hottentots. Finding themselves all at once released from the coercive shackles and oppressive disabilities to which their race had been so long subjected, a large portion, from a not unnatural impulse, left the service of the colonists as soon as their contracts of servitude expired, and some even fancied themselves authorised by the new law to break short those engagements. Many repaired to missionary institutions (which but few had been previously permitted to enter), without having adequate means to maintain themselves there. Numbers flocked to the district towns and villages, where the temptations of cheap brandy, procurable by little labour, soon betrayed many into profligate habits, and led some of them to commit depredations on the flocks of the farmers.[17]

Pringle explains that these actions were not restrained because many wished, or the evidence suggested they wished, to be able to point to the failure of the new act and thus to exert pressure for its repeal. Then word arrived from England which made impossible any return of the old legal condition. At this time, Pringle says, officials moved into action: "the partial disorders, naturally occurring under such circumstances, were found to be very easily repressed by the ordinary police of the country, when due diligence was used to effect this object; while the quiet and orderly conduct of the great body of the Hottentot people furnished the best practical refutation of those who had represented the whole race as unfit for the enjoyment of rational liberty."[18] Finally, Pringle concludes, "The great body of the Hottentot people still remained, in fact, just as they were formerly, servants to the white colonists, though with some essential differences in their condition."[19] He ends by saying that his information from the Cape indicated that great moral improvement might be seen developing in the race.

Next, with very obvious satisfaction, Pringle relates an experiment attempted in 1829. The government decided to settle Hottentots in an area which was to belong to them alone. Late in June, midwinter, some two hundred and fifty families were settled upon a tract of wild country just north of Fort Beaufort. Because a Bantu chief, Makomo, had recently been expelled from this area, it was feared that reprisals might be expected. For this reason the Hottentots were given guns and ammunition, which caused cries of alarm from many, who insisted that the arms would be turned against Europeans. What happened, or the essential part, is told by Pringle in one paragraph.

. . . The principal families, among whom were the whole of our former Mulatto tenants from Glen-Lynden, possessed a considerable quantity of live stock; but there were great numbers who were totally destitute of property of any description,—destitute even of food for daily subsistence. Yet under these circumstances, although no aid whatever was given them by Government, except arms for their defence and a very small portion of seed-corn, even the most destitute abstained from theft—a crime to which in their servile state they are said by some (though I think unjustly) to have been prone. Those who had cattle assisted their poorer friends and relatives with a generous liberality which is characteristic of the race. Those who had neither food nor friends, lived upon *veld-kost,* i.e., wild roots and bulbs dug out of the soil, until the land they had planted returned them a harvest. Multitudes subsisted in this manner without a murmur for many months. Extraordinary industry was at the same time exerted. With the most wretched implements they cultivated an extent of land which astonished every one; and, independently of the labour required in culture, the various parties displayed extraordinary rivalship in the construction of canals to convey water for the irrigation of their fields and gardens. In some places those canals were carried through the solid rock; in others it was necessary to cut to the depth of ten or twelve feet to preserve the level; while their entire length through all the locations extended to upwards of 20,000 yards. Meanwhile they had sustained many fierce attacks from the Caffers, generally made in the dead of night, and had bravely repulsed them, without ever indulging the spirit of retaliation or repaying evil for evil. When the winter was over the Caffers ceased to harass the locations, and the neighbouring chiefs, especially Makomo who had been driven out of this territory, ere long entered into the most friendly relations with the settlers. Their industry having been rewarded with an abundant harvest, especially of vegetables, their numbers continued constantly to increase by fresh accessions of their countrymen, until they at length amounted altogether to upwards of four thousand souls, of whom about seven hundred were armed with muskets.[20]

For five years Pringle followed the progress of the Kat River settlement and at the end of his chapter adds a note saying he has received a letter (after the material had been set in type and was going to press) bringing his information up to 1834. The pride which Pringle felt in this venture was very great. Certainly, part of this resulted from the fact that his family tenants were among the Hottentot settlers, but much of his reaction came from that desire in him to see justice done and human beings free.

Though Pringle's chapter on the Bantu tribes of the Cape is much the longest in his book, it is inadequate for what he has attempted to do. Here, for the first time, he is trying to write general history. The relation between the Europeans and the Bantu peoples was the great problem of South Africa. As has been explained, the 1820 Settlers had not understood before they left England that they were being brought to the Cape for military reasons first, economic ones second, and others beyond these. War between the European and Bantu groups was an established fact, but the sorting out of the details was an extremely difficult task. Perhaps somewhat inadvertently Pringle reveals his situation in the initial paragraphs of this chapter. "My residence of nearly three years on the eastern frontier naturally led me to pay considerable attention to the character of our colonial relations with the Caffer tribes; and my intimacy with several intelligent officers who had had much intercourse with those tribes both in peace and war, as well as with missionaries long resident among them, having enabled me to acquire information on many points which my own limited opportunities of observation did not embrace, I shall endeavour to throw together in the present chapter a brief summary of my researches on this topic." [21]

Everywhere a historian turned in trying to present the total situation in South Africa during the nineteenth century, he encountered complexity. To begin with, there were the problems created by a country which for many generations had been in the hands of a Dutch commercial company and was now under control of the English Parliament. As soon as the new government attempted any kind of control, they had the Dutch Boers in opposition—along with the natives, who had before this period been in a state of continual war with the Boers. Increased complication came from the fact that officials in London, or even in Cape Town, knew very little about Bantu civilization, and therefore understood very little. Naturally there were mistakes of almost every variety, and these created confusion and conflicts. The *certainty* of the missionaries that they knew all and understood all was not very helpful in the tense situation which existed. Even if everyone involved was honest, hard working, and intent upon discovering the facts and reaching a true judgment, the problem would have been difficult to solve. Yet when man's greed, inefficiency, and natural prejudices are considered, it is hard to believe that anything can be done under such circumstances.

This, then, is the kind of historical period which Thomas Pringle attempted to survey in one chapter. About all that can be said is that he identified many of the conflicts, presented numerous actors in the events of the era, described some of the important happenings, and commented as he proceeded. A reader certainly feels that he has learned many things about the place and the time. Pringle ended his account with an impassioned plea:

> . . . The Native Tribes . . . are ready to throw themselves into our arms. Let us open our arms cordially to embrace them as MEN and as BROTHERS. Let us enter upon a new and nobler career of conquest. Let us subdue savage Africa by JUSTICE, by KINDNESS, by the talisman of CHRISTIAN TRUTH. Let us *thus* go forth, in the name and under the blessing of God, gradually to extend the moral influence, and, if it be thought desirable, the territorial boundary also of our Colony, until it shall become an Empire—embracing Southern Africa from the Keisi and Gareep to Mozambique and Cape Negro—and to which, peradventure, in after days, even the equator shall prove no ultimate limit.[22]

Less than a year of life remained for Thomas Pringle after he wrote these words. Perhaps it was well that he did not see what was to happen in South Africa during the next century.

V *Pringle's Achievement in Prose*

Though it would be difficult to prove, one suspects that the immediate success of Thomas Pringle's *Narrative of a Residence in South Africa* resulted from the fact that the chapters on the native peoples appealed to a substantial audience at the moment. Continuing success certainly depended upon diversity and upon writing and materials which pleased a wide audience. Diversity, however, may be not only the weakness of the book but the ultimate weakness of Thomas Pringle the writer. He had a number of talents but permitted himself to develop fully none of them. His statement that he would "throw together" the chapter of the Bantu history in South Africa reveals clearly his attitude towards his prose work. Much of the volume derives from his journal and the late writing was of the kind discussed in Part IV of the present chapter. What Pringle needed was stern self-discipline which would force a rigorous concentration on what he did best and the exclusion of all that did not belong in a single book.

Perhaps it was asking the impossible to expect that Pringle, after seven years as secretary of the Anti-Slavery Society, could function again as an imaginative writer. Yet when one reads the early pages of the *Narrative,* knowing that much of this was recorded in his journal, open upon his knees, as the Pringles journeyed towards a new home, he is saddened in observing that this type of writing was abandoned fourteen years before the author completed his career. Here are two entries made at the end of the first day. The first gives a scene passed during the afternoon:

> This lake, which lies in the midst of an extensive plain, elevated considerably above the level of the sea, is of an oval form, about three miles in circumference, and has on one side a sloping margin of green turf; in other parts, banks of greater elevation and abruptness are covered with continuous thickets of arboreous and succulent plants. At the time of our visit the whole of the lake round the margin, and a considerable portion of its entire surface, was covered with a thick rind of salt sprinkled over with small snow-white crystals, giving the whole basin the aspect of a pond partially frozen and powdered over with hoar frost or flakes of snow. This wintry appearance of the lake formed a singular contrast with the exuberant vegetation which embowered its margins, where woods of beautiful evergreens and elegant acacias were intermingled with flowering shrubs and succulent plants of lofty size and strange exotic aspect,—such as the *Portulacaria afra* (favorite food of the elephant), the tree *crassula,* the scarlet *cotelydon,* with several species of the *aloe,* some of them of large size, and in summer crested with superb tiaras of blood-red blossoms; and, high over all, gigantic groves of *euphorbia,* extending their leafless arms above the far-spread forest of shrubbery. The effect of the whole, flushed with a rosy tinge by the setting sun, was singularly striking and beautiful.[23]

The second entry calls attention to what was done after they stopped for the night:

It was not a little amusing after supper (as I sat in front of my wagon jotting down in my note book the day's memoranda) to contemplate the characteristic groups which our rustic camp exhibited. The Dutch-African boors, most of them men of almost gigantic size, sat apart in their bushy *bield* [shelter], in aristocratic exclusiveness, smoking their huge pipes with self-satisfied complacency. Some of the graver emigrants were seated on the trunk of a decayed tree, conversing in broad Scotch on subjects connected with our settlement, and on the comparative merits of long and short-horned cattle (the horns of the native oxen, by the way, are enormous): and the livelier young men and servant lads were standing round the Hottentots, observing their merry pranks, or practising with them a lesson of mutual tuition in their respective dialects; while the awkward essays at pronunciation on either side supplied a fund of ceaseless entertainment. Conversation appeared to go on with alacrity, though neither party understood scarcely a syllable of the other's language; while a sly rogue of a Bushman sat behind, all the while, mimicking, to the very life, each of us in succession. These groups, with all their variety of mien and attitude, character and complexion,—now dimly discovered, now distinctly lighted up by the fitful blaze of the watchfires. . . .

By degrees, the motley groups became hushed, under the influence of slumber. The settlers retired to their tents or their wagons; the boors, sticking their pipes in the bands of their broad-brimmed hats, wrapt themselves in their great coats, and, fearless of snake or scorpion, stretched their limbs on the bare ground; while the Hottentots, drawing themselves each under his sheep-skin *caross*, lay coiled up, with their feet to the fire and their faces to the ground, like so many hedgehogs. Over the wide expanse of wilderness, now reposing under the midnight moon, profound silence reigned,—unbroken save by the deep breathing of the oxen round the wagons, and, at times, by the far-off melancholy howl of a hyaena, the first voice of a beast of prey we had heard since our landing.[24]

In the first pasage, Pringle has convinced his reader that the salt lake existed, not because the recorder said it was there but because the reader himself has seen it. The second passage is even more useful as evidence. He has not only handled setting with economy but has shown several groups of people in the process of being human. Choice of detail here was much more difficult than in the first passage because of the multiplicity of facts among which he was forced to decide. The selection is, of course, for purposes of character development. The author also displays a definite sense of the dramatic as he depicts the little group engaged in a language lesson. The Bushman in the background is a felicitous bit, and the hedgehog image introduced with ease. By the time the moon looks down upon the scene, the reader is sure the whole camp is sleeping. If Thomas Pringle had developed to the limit skills exhibited here, his *Narrative* might have secured a high place in literature. With few if any exceptions, the narrative parts of the book are timeless. Always ephemeral, however, is any book or part of a book which espouses a cause. If the cause is won, the writing is dead because it has served its purpose. If the cause is lost, it has never really lived—at least in one sense. The clear implication is that parts of Pringle's book still live and other parts do not, except as history.

Another skill which Pringle might have used to even greater advantage than he did was in the handling of fact. He first exhibited this skill in presenting the physical details of the country which he initially saw as the *Brilliant* sailed to its place in Simon's Bay. Thomas had a passion for climbing mountains, and again and again he records details at the top or from the top. Here is what he said about the highest elevation in the Cape Province:

> . . . The temperature of the Sneeuwberg was at this season very cold, and all the higher points were covered with snow. The loftiest peak, called Compass-Berg, is considered, according to the most accurate estimate yet made, to be 6,500 feet above the level of the sea [actually 8,200]. The aspect of this elevated region was bleak, rugged, and bare of wood; but well watered, and, for Africa, rich in pasturage. It consists of a sort of plateau or table-land, rising abruptly from the plains of Camdeboo and the Karroo in immense buttresses of naked rock; the ledges or strata of which, . . . are so perfectly horizontal, and so regularly squared at the angles that but for their vast height and magnitude they might be taken for gigantic lines of masonry. The uppermost stratum consists of sandstone, intermingled, at intervals, with quartz: the bases are schistus. There is no appearance of granite. The soil on the summit is a stiff clay, thickly strewed with loose stones, but bearing, where it can be irrigated, good crops of wheat and barley. There is no timber, and scarcely a thicket of brushwood throughout the whole of the Sneeuwberg; so that the inhabitants are mostly obliged to use, for fuel, either a very small shrub (*stoebe rhinocerotis*), or the dung of their cattle, dried like turf, and to bring timber for building either from the coast or from the forests of Glen-Lynden and the Kaha.[25]

Because the passage quoted above has almost no utilitarian value and creates in the reader no ideological bias, it is an excellent example in which to examine Pringle's use of fact. Though organization exists, it achieves its puropse without calling attention to itself. Details are plentiful, but still selective and therefore the basis for economy. The primary intent of the paragraph is not to create an image, yet the reader receives a clear impression of the area. Here, indeed, is an instrument which Pringle used often, as illustrated a number of times in the present study. One can only wish that more time had been permitted him to employ this talent and his other abilities. The wish now being expressed means more than additional years in which to write. It is a wish that he had been relieved of some of the extreme pressures (one of them economic) which must often have kept him from doing his best.

Perhaps at no time in his life was Thomas Pringle's mind as completely freed from pressure as during the two years at Glen-Lynden, in what he called the wilds of Africa. Despite constant physical danger and hard bodily labor, his mind appears to have been released from debilitating tensions. This seems to have been the important germinal period. Much of the best work of his life was conceived between the moment he first saw land at Simon's Bay and the sight of Cape Town the second time as he descended from the heights of the mountain passes after a passage of the Karroo. During that period of a few days less than twenty-nine months the images and ideas which would become the foundation for his literary life had filled his mind.

CHAPTER 9

The End Is Decreed

TO the very end, Thomas Pringle's life was a series of reversals. When after years of waiting, he had been able to see a major prose work published; and when after all of his efforts, he was ready to present the world with a comprehensive collection of his poems; and when after his devoted service to the Anti-Slavery Society, he was to see abolition become a fact; at last when all seemed to be going right, he glanced up and saw death only a short distance before him. Though he was certainly not afraid to die and passed fully conscious and with great calmness, his writing life was ended just when the future seemed to offer what he had wanted.

Sight of blood which would soon reveal to Pringle what was ahead, he attributed at first to a coughing spell precipitated by swallowing a crumb "the wrong way," as it is always expressed. Because the coughing appeared to have left effects, Pringle wrote the next morning to his doctor. The patient was, however, quickly beyond the help of the best medical knowledge of 1834. Spitting of blood continued, and he lost weight and strength. Soon it was evident that racing tuberculosis had gripped him. As the English winter threatened, doctors advised the only thing they knew—find a milder climate. The medical specialist called even identified the Cape as one of the best places for the disease. Instantly Pringle's mind turned to the South African sun, and he commenced almost frantic efforts to raise funds and prepare for the trip. Friends in the Anti-Slavery Society provided enough to get him to South Africa at once. Pringle's request for land in the Cape was refused by the government, but letters were offered in his behalf, passage was booked, and preparations were hastened. Speed was necessary because the disease was progressing obviously. The sailing of his ship was delayed; and when it was ready, Thomas was too ill to risk starting. Doctors were of the opinion that he was not likely to reach Cape Town. Thus he remained in England and awaited the end which he knew was coming. There was no great delay. On December 5, 1834, he died. He was buried at Bunhill Fields, London, exactly a month before his forty-sixth birthday.

Though Thomas Pringle had hoped his biography would be written by John Fairbairn, he had depended upon one of the most complete procrastinators the world has ever known. Pringle's admiration for Fairbairn is one characteristic no student of the relation between the two men seems to have understood. Consistent to the end, Fairbairn wrote no biography, though he had known Pringle for more than twenty years and Thomas had furnished specific material for the work. It was Pringle's friends in London who wrote memoirs—Josiah Conder for an edition of the *Narrative* (1835) and Leitch Ritchie for an edition of the poems (1838). The first of these is some twenty-five pages and the second almost a hundred and fifty. For more than a century Conder and Ritchie were merely repeated in the various sketches of Pringle. Finally, a biography appeared, in 1968, and appropriately from the Cape. The book is *Thomas Pringle, His Life and Times,* by Jane Meiring. One of the most important facts about this study is the author's use of the letters Pringle wrote to Fairbairn. It may be that at last the spirit of one small Scot will begin to find some peace.

With two famous exceptions and considerable known criticism, much of the comment upon Pringle as a writer came after his death. Reference has already been made to the admiration expressed by Sir Walter Scott for Pringle's first major poem and how this turned into a literary connection which was used for personal reasons when Thomas undertook to sponsor the move in getting his family to South Africa. The second was also personal, a letter from Coleridge, which told the author about the elderly poet's discovery of "Afar in the Desert." Coleridge wrote, "I do not hesitate to declare it, among the two or three most perfect lyric poems in our language." [1] All evidence suggests that Pringle was deeply moved by the praise of these men, but he certainly longed for broader recognition. This could hardly have come before 1834, when the major work of his life was published, only months before his death. It should be remembered that *African Sketches* contained not only the prose *Narrative* but also the poems from South Africa. For the first time readers were able to see some bulk, and it seems reasonable to assume that many who purchased the volume because of an interest in one part found themselves being captivated by other sections. Soon, however, the prose and poetry were to be separated and again forced to make their way alone. Next, the poems of Scotland were dropped and the South African poems appeared as a single book because it was South Africa that was helping keep his name alive in the world of poetry. Finally, in the twentieth century, even in a South African edition, the poems of Scoland returned, and readers received all of Pringle's verse.

Meanwhile, evaluation had begun. In *The Quarterly Review* for December, 1835, a critic, believed to be J. G. Lockhart, reviewed *African Sketches* and had the following to say: "Pringle was a man of great worth, and of very considerable literary talents; an honest, warm-hearted man, in whom woeful physical deformities had been unable to chill the natural current of the benevolent affections—kindly, generous, and high of spirit—an enthusiastic philanthropist—in the purest sense of the all-comprehending word, a Christian. No one can consider either his earliest or his latest publications without feeling that he had in him some sparks of true genius. . . . He wrote many verses while in Africa—and by these he will be, at all events, remembered among the colonists; but he little deserves to be forgotten elsewhere. What strikes us as most remarkable in Pringle's poetry is its almost constant elegance . . . there is rarely in his prose, and almost never in his verse, anything with which the most fastidious reader can have the smallest right to be offended. We think the Evening Rambles in their style almost faultless. . . . Pringle could sound a more stirring note. . . . But we really could have formed no notion until we read these sketches, of the gallant and heroic daring of which Pringle in his own feeble person was capable, when thrown among scenes of excitement and peril, or how well his verse could keep pace with such ardours." [2]

Because Pringle's death coincided so closely with publication of the two major works of his life, it was only natural that those who commented would speak of the man as well as the work. In his memoir, unabashedly a hymn of praise, written for the first complete edition of Pringle's poems, Leitch Ritchie said that "The death of Thomas Pringle drew forth an expression of affectionate regret in every civilised country in the world where the English language is spoken. In British India, in America, in Africa, the feeling was the same; and to the credit of human nature be it related, that even his adversaries joined in lamenting when dead the man they had striven against when living. The eulogiums pronounced by contemporary writers would fill a volume of themselves. . . ." [3] Josiah Conder, who in writing his, the first of the Pringle memoirs, who was beside him during the author's illness and at the moment of death, commented: "The name of Thomas Pringle deserves to be held in affectionate remembrance as that of a benefactor, in more than one region of the globe. Without power, without wealth, his abilities were so well directed, and the providential circumstances of his life, harmonising with the purity of his views, afforded such wide scope for his modest, but efficient labours, that posterity will be largely his debtor. How few among the number of those who have devoted themselves to literary employments, have lived for so good a purpose, and left behind so unsullied a name! There was in Mr. Pringle's whole course, a sort of dramatic propriety, which eminently marked its close: he died in the field of usefulness, at the moment that his specific work seemed to be done." [4] At the beginning of his memoir, Leitch Ritchie made it very definite why he felt that the mingling of details about Pringle's conduct as a human being and whatever he wrote must be inevitable, regardless of the time at which the comments were made. "He was never, at any period of his life, a mere author. Literature, with him, was inseparably connected with the practical amelioration of the human race—it was the armour he assumed in the great struggle of civilization. This was the case throughout his whole career, although more apparent to the public in the latter years of his life; when, owing to his double position as a literary man, and the Secretary of the Anti-Slavery Society, he formed the connecting link between the press and the sacred cause of freedom—or, if I may use the expression in a restricted sense—between the moral and intellectual world." [5]

Though he protested his belief in the union of two worlds in the man named Thomas Pringle, Leitch Ritchie quite naturally gave most of his pages to the person rather than to what he wrote. At the end of his biographical study, he attempts to focus in two pages his reaction to a man he had known intimately:

One of the gentlest yet firmest, one of the humblest yet most high-minded of human beings, the character of Thomas Pringle was made up of qualities, which excite in equal proportions affection and respect. With him benevolence was not a weakness, but a principle. He did not *indulge* in doing good; but his humanity, being under the strict control of his judgment, he refuted practically the doctrines of that philosophy which refers even our best actions to selfishness. He was warm and steady in his attachments; but though he would have risked his life for his friend, he would not have sacrificed his probity. He was deeply religious, but not of those devotees who "crucify their countenances." Cheerful, buoyant, and even gay, he exemplified his faith only in his actions. Open, generous, manly, and sincere. . . .

In person he was rather under than over the middle size, apparently in consequence of his lower limbs having been prevented by the accident I have mentioned from acquiring their due development. His body was well formed; his head strikingly intellectual; and his face characterised by an expression of mingled sweetness and sagacity, not common in their union. He was rather what is termed good-looking than strictly handsome; but his eye, which knew how to kindle as well as melt, to upbraid as well as soothe, threw such gleams of sentiment over his countenance as would have redeemed much more common features.

How did it happen that engaged as he was, through his whole life, in a continued moral struggle, "no man (as a critic remarks) ever had fewer enemies, or descended into the grave with fewer animosities?" The explanation is to be found in his singleness of heart and purpose, in that *whiteness of soul* which, even when brought into contact with impurity, threw off the stains of the world, as if by some natural law of repulsion. Perhaps—but on this subject I dare not enter—perhaps we may trace the steadfastness of his mind to higher causes, to nobler principles: perhaps we may account for the unity presented in his life, by the fact of his moral energies being continually under the direction and control of his religious convictions. . . .[6]

After leaving behind in the history of the period all of the emotion which initially prompted Leitch Ritchie to write the memoir, after abandoning the abstractions and praise words, after putting in abeyance his theory, there is still a very significant claim being made. Often within himself Thomas Pringle seemed to possess unity when the world around him was composed of warring elements. Without questioning, yet without employing Ritchie's explanation founded upon the influence of supernatural power, the reader may wish to recall some of the elements that went into the equation for which a solution is being sought.

Until into his teens, Pringle was emerging from an environment which kept him minutely in touch with the world of physical actuality: soil, crops, weather, animals, birds; flowers, trees, streams; fences, barns, houses. This was the environment in which he—as another physical fact—lived. With very little danger of opposition, it may be claimed that the religion which existed in this environment was almost as solid a fact as the soil, the streams, and the houses. Landscape, stories, and beliefs were all familiar. Then, for Thomas, change came. Latin was learned at the Kelso Grammar School. Edinburgh and the university offered the world of literature and ideas—the outside world in a state of violent flux. The usual way of referring to what has happened is to explain that a farm boy has become a university man, or a city man, which is likely to suggest that the university-trained mind has lost the heritage bestowed by the land. There may be instances in which this happens, but the evidence available in relation to Thomas Pringle demonstrates that he added but never subtracted. It was said of him that whenever he returned to the country for a vacation, he was loath to leave it. Slightly later, trained now in the world of literature, he made his first major poem a celebration of the rural scenes among which he grew up. Having mastered the English of an enviable prose style and an elegant poetic one, he clung in theory and fact to his Scottish speech whenever he was allowed to use it.

As long as Thomas was in Edinburgh, none of this seemed worthy of remark. Once at Glen-Lynden, however, everything implies that the characteristic is indeed worthy of examination. Among the Pringle party it was Thomas—and *only* Thomas—who carried within himself the two worlds which the settlers from Scotland definitely needed in their new home. At Cape Town, Algoa Bay, Roodewal, and finally when they reached Baviaans River, it was Thomas who conferred with government and military officials and gave the answers which turned the Pringles in the direction of success—rather than the failure suffered by many groups. While it was Thomas who handled the written communications for the party and who was able to meet with the acting governor and other important persons, significant advantage came to his father and family because of the knowledge which their representative had of soil, water supply, crops, animals, and building. He was not merely the secretary and spokesman for the group; he understood the situation being considered. In addition to being able to work with important officials, he had the human qualities which made successful his relations with the Hottentots, with the Boers, and indeed with the vast variety of human beings he met in South Africa. In many ways, this is the most revealing and significant fact about Thomas Pringle. It was the characteristic which developed in him profound sympathy for the oppressed but made it possible for him to understand their oppressors. Again it was the union within himself of the abstract and the concrete. Freedom and justice were the two great *ideas* of his life, but there was another quality which made him acutely aware of the individual actuality of human beings. Thus, when he hated actions that destroyed freedom and refused justice, he could simultaneously be aware of *other* kinds of actions by those same individuals. These other acts displayed human kindness, generosity, love—many characteristics he could admire. Ultimately, his feeling of sadness was for the vast and profound contradictions found in mankind.

Certainly one of the most accurate ways to identify that in Pringle which made him what Leitch Ritchie claimed is by examining the reaction to him of a wide range of people. As the first witness, one might call Robert Story. The fathers of Robert and Thomas had arranged for the boys to attend the university together. Before starting for Edinburgh, Robert had come to spend the night at the Pringles', for the boys had never met. After the elders had gone off to bed, the young men sat before the fire and talked and also later from their beds, long into the night. Of the friendship which started at this time, Story wrote, "His warmth of affection, his ingenuousness, and his integrity were, at the very commencement of our fellowship, as truly revealed to me in his sayings and doings, as if I had known him for years." [7] For Robert Story to be receptive to a son of his father's friend was rather to be expected in 1802; but the moment Thomas Pringle arrived in South Africa, he was among strangers. Yet they too must have trusted Thomas. In June, 1821, he conferred with Sir Rufane Donkin, acting governor of the Cape, concerning the enlargement of the grants of land to the Pringle party. As a result of this conference, the holdings of the group were increased by about eighteen times. Evidently Sir Rufane was impressed. Another man who showed an early interest in Thomas was Robert Hart, superintendent of the Government Farm at Somerset East. He was one of the first men in the country to invite Pringle to travel with him on some of his movements throughout the Eastern Cape. That he should have invited a man who could only move with the aid of crutches suggests that he saw something else to which he was responding. As a final example in this area, one might name Captain Sir Andries Stockenstrom, with whom he made an extended visit not long before leaving South Africa. One of the most remarkable men to enter Pringle's life, Captain Stockenstrom left no slight influence upon the still young man who sailed back to England.

Though a very long list of men from Scotland, South Africa, and England could be compiled to show that Thomas Pringle had something that created confidence, the examples already given should establish the attitudes held by most with whom he had any close contact. To all of this there was one exception. Never at any time did Thomas Pringle approve of men who used political power to oppress human beings. In this whole area Pringle seemingly refused to accept such people. To them, unlike other persons, he refused balancing characteristics. Perhaps a legitimate guess is that he considered the power they used belonged initially to the people, and for such oppression there was no grace.

Much was said during Pringle's life and immediately after concerning the reaction of the defenseless and unfortunate to this man who gave seven years of his life to the freeing of slaves—with his mind constantly focused upon his experiences in South Africa. The mention of South Africa is not only accurate but as events have demonstrated the proper historical direction. It is South Africa that kept his memory alive in the way that he longed to be known—as the author of a collection of poems.

CHAPTER 10

South African Poetry in English

I *The Beginning*

QUITE literally, South African poetry in English emerged in 1822 from the imagination of Thomas Pringle as he sat in summer weather beneath an umbra tree beside his cabin at Baviaans River. Thomas was writing to his friend John Fairbairn, who from Newcastle-on-Tyne had no other way of viewing the interior areas of the Eastern Cape. Letters to Fairbairn, however, in at least one practical sense, served little purpose, since John seldom responded. Why not, then, abandon the pretense of practicality and create a poem? Following his impulse, Pringle began to write in verse of his cabin and the strange new scenes around him. He called the result "The Emigrant's Cabin," which upon publication he subtitled "An Epistle in Rhyme." What he initiated that day should not pass unnoticed. Pringle had composed earlier poems using African material. A sonnet, "Enon," written in April, 1821, had recorded his reaction to a Moravian Mission Station visited at that time. This regular Italian sonnet, however, with traditional diction, certainly did not contribute very much to the development of South African poetry.

Though in its original version "The Emigrant's Cabin" was written in 1822, Pringle did not send the letter to Fairbairn but placed the lines among his papers and took the poem with him to England, where it was to be revised and published in *Poems Illustrative of South Africa*, 1834, which was Part I of *African Sketches*. From London, May 22, 1834, Pringle wrote to Fairbairn concerning this poem which had started as a letter to John. "You will be surprised to find yourself *hitched* into rhyme in a long piece of verse you have never seen. The fact is that on turning over my old scraps one day I found the rough commencement of a rhyming epistle to you, the germ or embrio of what you now see, & which I had begun, but never sent to you, & indeed had entirely forgotten. I set to & with little labour extended it to the thing you now see—(not the worst of my attempts in my own opinion)—and retaining the original *date*, I managed by a little anachronism to bring in the Dr. [Dr. John Philip] & other friends. I really think it improves my African collection considerably by giving a view of our familiar & domestic condition. My friend & neighbour the Wizard Coleridge is very fond if it." [1]

Writing to John Fairbairn from London in 1834, Thomas Pringle probably grasped more completely the value of "The Emigrant's Cabin" than was possible on South African soil in 1822. The modest claim that it is "not the worst of [his] attempts" and "will improve [his] African collection" suggests a rather definite assurance of its worth. Coleridge's support, of course, bolstered his satisfaction with what he had written. The most substantial evidence of all is the fact that he was willing to give this one piece fifteen pages among the South African poems which filled only a hundred and fourteen pages of his verse and prose book called *African Sketches.*

In diction and structure "The Emigrant's Cabin" was far more useful to future generations than a poem such as "Evening Rambles," also concerned with scenes of the Baviaans River settlement. The "Rambles" had been selected by the *Quarterly Review* critic as in a "style almost faultless," but everything about the style directed the reader back to poetry of the past and reminded him that this type of composition belonged to Europe. What was needed was writing that would focus attention upon South Africa, and this is exactly what the "Epistle" did. The method is dramatic: in fact this is the nearest thing to a play that Pringle wrote.

Setting exists in some detail because, as he composed, the author's mind was intent upon the actual scene which he wished to transmit to his friend thousands of miles away. What he has imagined is not the South African situation but the physical presence of John as he approaches the new home of Thomas, which he has never visited. As an author, Thomas undertakes first to depict what the visitor—were he present—would see, hear, touch, taste, and smell. When the action begins, the host is seated before his reed-thatched cabin situated upon a knoll, with a steep mountain behind. Beside his feet is his old hound Yarrow.

Thomas stands to welcome the guest and invites him into the house, with its uncarpeted and cool clean floor. For a seat he offers a jointed stool or a couch of leopard skin. While giving some approval to the cottage, Fairbairn considers the beehive shape odd. Then mention of dinner turns the conversation in the direction of things South Africa is able to provide for the table:

First, here's our broad-tailed mutton, small and fine,
The dish on which nine days in ten we dine;
Next, roasted springbok, spiced and larded well;
A haunch of hartèbeest from Hyndhope Fell;
A paauw, which beats your Norfolk turkey hollow;
Korhann, and Guinea-fowl, and pheasant, follow;
Kid carbonadjes, à-la-Hottentot,
Broiled on a forkèd twig; and, peppered hot
With Chili pods, a dish called Caffer-stew;
Smoked ham of porcupine, and tongue of gnu.
This fine white household bread (of M——t's baking)
Comes from an oven too of my own making,
Scooped from an ant-hill. Did I ask before
If you would taste this brawn of forest-boar?
. . . there's green roasted maize, and pumpkin pie,
And wild asparagus. Or will you try
A slice of water-melon?—fine for drouth,
Like sugared ices melting in the mouth.
Here too are wild-grapes from our forest-vine,
Not void of flavour, though unfit for wine.
And here comes dried fruit I had quite forgot,
(From fair Glen-Avon,M——t, is it not?)
Figs, almonds, raisins, peaches. Witbooy Swart
Brought this huge sackful from kind Mrs. Hart—
Enough to load a Covent-Garden cart.[2]

Ostensibly inviting his guest to dinner, actually Thomas is enumerating available foods. In addition he furnishes some information concerning methods of preparation and a few asides indicating source of supply and persons involved. Even the original impulse, however, must have transcended the desire to give his friend a mere list of food found in South Africa. Considerable competence is evident in the presentation of the things named. Skill in the handling of details is likewise revealed in another section as he explains the location of a member of the emigrant group living at some distance from the cottage which is the setting for this little play. Acted on a stage, Thomas would turn and point as he spoke these words: "Past that dark ravine,—/ Where on the left gigantic crags are seen,/ And the steep Tarka mountains, stern and bare,/ Close round the upland cleughs of lone Glen-Yair,—/ Our Lothian Friends with their good Mother dwell,/ Beside yon *Kranz* whose pictured records tell/ Of Bushmen's huntings in the days of old,/ Ere here Bezuidenhout had fixed his fold."[3] With a few more than fifty words, Pringle has created a setting with considerable depth. The painting mentioned identifies as originally Bushman country the area to which he points. The phrasing establishes the Bushmen not only as painters but as hunters. In naming one of the Dutch settlers who drove the native peoples from the area, Pringle refers to an important historical event. Bezuidenhout, his family, and friends rose in fanatical opposition to the coming of government into that territory, perhaps especially English government. Killed or captured, the Dutch were dispossessed of their lands, which were then used for the 1820 Settlers. It was to this area that the Pringle party had come. The particular grant to which Thomas points was settled by the widow Rennie and her children—George, John, Peter, and Elizabeth. Calling them Lothian friends explains the locality from which they came in Scotland, and Glen-Yair tells the reader that Scottish names have replaced the South African ones. *Kranz,* however, pulls the reader back to South Africa, though "cleughs" returns him to a word originally Middle English but one which would have been natural to Pringle. In fact, nothing here seems unnatural—nothing done for effect.

What had to be self-conscious, however, was the way in which he organized his materials. The guest is received and welcomed into the house. After a few remarks having to do with the room and furniture, the host announces the serving of dinner. Now the hostess and her sister appear and all are seated. In the scene the presence of a Hottentot serving girl is natural, along with the language in which she is addressed. Conversation and dinner proceed, until the ladies rise and leave the gentlemen, who continue their conversation. Immediately the visitor asks how his host is able to stand this existence of mere physicality, why he is content with shelter and food without "The feast of Reason and the flow of Soul?" In quick reply, Thomas reminds John that living in South Africa has not been without satisfaction and stimulation: he explains that he has found interests which keep him busy, he feels that what he is doing represents a contribution to mankind, and he argues in detail that his friends are not to be scorned. Captain Harding, he says, makes "shrewd remarks on things and men"; Landdrost Stockenstrom "Is able in affairs, in books well read"; the men and their wives (he names them) at Somerset and officers at Káha and Roodewál have been friendly and kind; Captain Fox is "gay-humoured"; and the missionaries from time to time visit and supply another need. He concludes with, "You see, even in my desert-den,/ I still hold intercourse with thinking men. . . ."[4]

At this moment Mrs. Pringle summons them to late afternoon tea, served in the open, before the house. Fairbairn notes the sunset sky and the cowherd's call as he approaches home from the mountain pasture. Suddenly he observes strange people upon the bank of the river. It is an Amatémbu chief from Zwort-Kei, with a party of armed warriors. They come, Thomas reassures his guest, upon a friendly visit, long promised. The old Hottentot shepherd who approaches to announce their arrival says, "Powána wagh/ Tot dat de Bass hem binnenshuis zal vraagh." This speech says that "Powána waits/ Till Master bid him welcome to our gates."[5] Pringle hastens to greet the new arrivals and to give instructions for their entertainment. Here the little play ends.

Not only has Thomas Pringle used the South African scene and employed minute detail, not only has he introduced local words and even whole speeches in a language of the country, but he has also written in defense of life in South Africa. Perhaps Pringle himself was not quite aware of how much of a South African he had become, and certainly he could not know how important his example would be to future writers.

II *The Emigrant*

Loss of home and friends was a fact that often claimed the concious part of Pringle's mind and moved him to insist upon his emigrant status and his love for Scotland. It will be remembered that in 1824 when the first number of the *South African Journal* appeared, Pringle as editor claimed that his own poem giving an emigrant's lament was among the earliest contributions of merit received from the settlers who had recently taken up positions on the frontier (see Chapter 4). Though he did not retain the poem in its original state, he finally used one which expressed much the same sentiments. There were basic changes, however, before the poem made its final appearances. The lament became that of a Scottish lass from Pringle's own home area rather than an English maid, and the choral stanza exchanged South African material for that of Scotland. In a note Pringle carefully explains that the feelings are the imagined ones of a "desolate female emigrant, when first placed in the midst of an African wilderness, [rather] than the real sentiments of any of the Scottish settlers in that vicinity." [6] The meaning here would seem to depend upon the word "real." Pringle appears to be suggesting that the sentiments are not those of an individual, as for example, Elizabeth Rennie, of his own party of settlers. Yet the sentiments were *true* ones and were certainly felt by many of the emigrants during that first year. The germinal moment of the poem may well have been Pringle's observations starting with what he encountered the first hours ashore at Algoa Bay. As he explored along the beach, he came upon families of obvious refinement, wealth, and even aristocratic rank. Immediately his mind plunged into the future and imagined these people settled in the interior of Africa. Concerning this situation, he pondered "How far they had acted wisely in embarking their property and the happiness of their families in an enterprise like the present, and in leading their respective bands of adventurers to colonise the wilds of Southern Africa, were questions yet to be determined. Foreseeing, as I did in some degree, (although certainly by no means to the full extent), the difficulties and privations inevitable in such circumstances, I could not view this class of emigrants, with their elegant arrangements and appliances, without some melancholy misgivings as to their future fate; for they appeared utterly unfitted by former habits, especially the females, for *roughing it* (to use the expressive phraseology of the camp) through the first trying period of the settlement." [7] Later, when he made a tour of the whole district with Mr. Hart, Pringle observed the fulfillment of what he had expected would happen. Writing lines which expressed a normal reaction of the emigrants was certainly to be expected, especially for a poet of Pringle's kind, who frequently worked directly from his environmental situation. This is precisely what he was doing when he composed other lines on the emigrants. The poem which he called "An Emigrant's Song" was essentially a statement of his emotions created by the success of his own family in the new home they had chosen.

Oh! Maid of the Tweed, wilt thou travel with me,
To the wilds of South Africa, far o'er the sea,
Where the blue mountains tow'r in the beautiful clime,
Hung round with huge forests all hoary with time?
I'll build thee a cabin beside the clear fount,
Where it leaps into light from the heart of the mount,
Ere yet its fresh footsteps have found the fair meads
Where among the tall lilies the antelope feeds.

Our home, like a bee-hive, shall stand by the wood
Where the lory and turtle-dove nurse their young brood,
And the golden-plumed paroquet waves his bright wings
From the bough where the green-monkey gambols and swings;
With the high rocks behind us, the valley before,
The hills on each side with our flocks speckled o'er,
And the far-sweeping river oft glancing between,
With the heifers reclined on its margins of green.

There, rich in the wealth which a bountiful soil
Pours forth to repay the glad husbandman's toil;
Content with the Present, at peace with the Past,
No cloud on the Future our joys to o'ercast;
Like our brave Scottish sires in the blithe Olden Day,
The heart will keep young though the temples wax gray;
While love's Olive Plants round our table shall rise—
Engrafted with Hopes that bear fruit in the Skies.[8]

This is the style and these are the sentiments heretofore associted with Scotland. Phrased as an invitation and promise for the future, the lines actually identify the Pringle location at Baviaans River, and the "Content with the Present, at peace with the Past,/ No cloud on the Future. . . ." expresses satisfaction with the course of events. Though the literary weakness of the poem is obvious, Pringle's acceptance of South Africa determined the kind of poetry he wrote. An author from Scotland who composed poems while living in South Africa would be almost meaningless to the literary future of the country, but an author writing with approval of the land was likely to receive acceptance from that land. Not only time after time, but in various ways, Thomas Pringle demonstrated his acceptance of much that belonged to Africa's far south, and because he could give he was finally to receive.

III *The Native Peoples*

When the *Brilliant* brought Thomas Pringle into Algoa Bay, May 15, 1820, it came to anchor with the *Aurora,* which had carried Thomas Slater, great-grandfather of Francis Carey Slater, who three quarters of a century later dedicated himself to carrying on in poetry some of the things Pringle had started. One of the important aspects of Slater's work is the "Dark Folk" collection, started it seems about 1902 and given its final form in 1935. Though there is no resemblance in style and method and the details of subject matter between what Pringle and Slater wrote, the use of the native peoples in serious literature was an important common practice. It is perhaps even more significant that each man approached the "Dark Folk" as people rather than as promising literary objects. On his father's farm, young Slater had known through daily contacts the natives Pringle called Caffers. Both men had lived in the Xhosa area, though to Pringle the Caffers were dangerous enemies rather than the farm laborers that Slater knew. Both, however, wrote because of an interest. Pringle was interested in setting them free and saving their souls: Slater was interested in saving a record of their customs and language.

When Pringle arranged his South African poems for publication with the *Narrative,* 1834, he placed first his lines on "The Bechuana Boy." This also came first in the collected poems which he was planning at the time of his death. Everything suggests that this poem was very important to him, especially the long note he offered at the time of publication. What the author did was give the background history which prompted the composition.

> *"Ik ben alleenig in de waereld!"* was the touching expression of Marossi, the Bechuana orphan boy, in his broken Dutch, when he first fell accidentally under my protection, at Milk River in Camdebóo, in September 1825. He was then apparently about nine or ten years of age, and had been carried off from his native country by the

Bergenaars. He was sold to a Boor (for an old jacket!), only a few months previously, when the kraal or hamlet of his tribe had been sacked by those banditti in the manner described in the text. The other incidents of the poem are also taken from his own simple narrative, with the exception of his flying to the desert with a tame springbok—a poetical license suggested to me by seeing, a few days afterwards, a slave child playing with a springbok fawn at a boor's residence.

This little African accompanied my wife and me to England; and with the gradual development of his feelings and faculties he became interesting to us in no ordinary degree. He was indeed a remarkable child. With a great flow of animal spirits and natural hilarity, he was at the same time docile, observant, reflective, and always unselfishly considerate of others. He was of a singularly ingenuous and affectionate disposition; and, in proportion as his reason expanded, his heart became daily more thoroughly imbued with the genuine spirit of the gospel, insomuch that all who knew him involuntarily and with one consent, applied to this African boy the benignant words of our Saviour—"Of such is the Kingdom of Heaven." He was baptized in 1827, and took on himself (in conjunction with Mrs. P. and me), his baptismal vows, in the most devout and sensible manner. Shortly afterwards he died of a pulmonary complaint under which he had for many months suffered with exemplary meekness.[9]

Few compositions which came from the mind of Thomas Pringle reveal more completely the man and poet than "The Bechuana Boy." To begin with, he satisfied very deeply his humanitarian impulse in being able to free Marossi from slavery, to give him a home, and to replace cruelty with kindness. Then, almost immediately, he offered religious instruction, had seen baptism administered, and at the time of death been certain that he had brought salvation to the boy's soul. All of this was totally extraliterary and existed outside of any wish to convert experience into poetry. Yet it is accurate to describe Thomas Pringle as essentially an "experience poet." Most of what he wrote emerged directly from what he was doing. More significant, the best of his work was that which was closest to him as an experienced fact or emotion—the second frequently a direct extension of the first. This statement describes the process which brought "The Bechuana Boy" into being as a poem.

Following his meeting with Marossi, September 1825, and receiving him into the home, Pringle wrote a poem about the boy and during October sent it to Fairbairn in Cape Town. In his letter he commented that the style was "adapted to please a class of readers whom you too much neglect . . . I mean women, children, counting house clerks, country functionaries & Aides de Camp, etc. This imitation of nursery poetry will I hope please them & you. Joking apart, I have tried this *very simple* style with something [word obliterated] a further view—to excite some sympathy in *very common* readers, for this class of unfortunate strangers—about 5 or 6 hundred of whom have lately been distributed in this quarter of the Colony. Nor is my little tale altogether fictitious." [10] Here is another example which suggests that when Pringle felt he was being the least exalted, the least poetic, he usually created that which was better than his most serious efforts. Writing for what he calls "*very common* readers," he offers first a narrative. As Chaucer had remarked, a common audience can remember a story. The following is the narrative Pringle offered his reader. Marossi, a Bechuana boy of nine or ten, approached Thomas Pringle's tent on the edge of the desert and asked to become his servant. According to the account, his kraal beyond the Stormberg is attacked by Bergenaars, marauding bands of mountain dwellers, who kill every man, burn the huts, and take the women, children, and herds captive. Three days they are driven without food or water. Many die. When they reach a great river, they rush into it to drink. They are forced across the stream, and under this pressure still others die. Beyond the river, those who had survived are sold as slaves. Marossi is parted from his mother and little sister. He attacks his "masters" only to be dashed upon the earth and bound. Now a slave and without companionship, he rescues a fawn from wild dogs. The animal comes to love Marossi, but his Boer master takes the fawn and gives it to his own child. In the darkness of the night, Marossi retrieves the animal and together they flee into the desert. Finally, he places himself at the mercy of Thomas Pringle.

Though few readers are likely to be unmoved by the narrative Pringle has written, the author made a special effort to give the story a dramatic frame and development. The events are presented orally by Marossi as he stands before the person to whom he is offering himself. From a Bushman he had heard about Pringle and had approached with these words as his final plea: "Because they say, O English Chief,/ Thou scornest not the Captive's grief:/ Then let me serve thee, as thine own—/ For I am in the world alone!"[11]

Because he had planned to reach a broad section of humanity, Pringle could be expected to introduce lyric qualities into his poem. Accordingly, he cast his effort in eight-line stanzas, using four rhymes, alternate in the first half and couplets in the second. The following lines will illustrate the direction in which the author was focusing his attention:

At length was heard a river sounding
  'Midst that dry and dismal land,
And, like a troop of wild deer bounding,
  We hurried to its strand—
Among the maddened cattle rushing;
The crowd behind still forward pushing,
Till in the flood our limbs were drenched,
And the fierce rage of thirst was quenched.

Hoarse-roaring, dark, the broad Gareep
  In turbid streams was sweeping fast,
Huge sea-cows in its eddies deep
  Loud snorting as we passed;
But that relentless robber-clan
Right through those waters wild and wan
Drove on like sheep our wearied band:
—Some never reached the farther strand.[12]

Pondering the phrasing of these stanzas, a reader is likely to shake his head and murmur, "for '*very common* readers?'" A negative shake, for the answer is "No, certainly not!" That Pringle was trying to develop a simple style is true, but it was not for "*very common* readers." There seems little doubt that his wish was to reach a wider audience than could be expected if the appeal was through traditional poetic methods. Late in 1825 Pringle was trying, without total success, to give up poetry and turn to a life devoted to the native races. This is the impulse which created the present poem. Even the most casual reading will reveal lines that were certainly composed for a special emotional effect: "wolfish howl of joy. . . . The slaughter o'er, they gave the slain/ To feast the foul-beaked birds of prey. . . . Behind us, on the desert brown,/ We saw the vultures swooping down:/

And heard, as the grim night was falling,/ The wolf to his gorged comrade calling. . . . When, with proud looks and gestures rude,/ The White Men gathered round:/ And there, like cattle from the fold,/ By Christians we were bought and sold. . . . And tears and toil have been my lot/ Since I the White Man's thrall became. . . . I rescued it, though wounded sore/ and dabbled in its mother's gore. . . ." [13] The intention here is clear: in South Africa the animal and human world are operating at the same level. The images depicting action, quoted above, are drawn almost exclusively from the animal world. When he turns to the question of slavery, it becomes a fact of color—though it is only when white enters that he names a color. In the process of capturing slaves, it is black against black; in buying them, it is black and white making a trade.

Quite interesting and very important was Pringle's use of the springbok, which was no part of Marossi's story—though it is used in the poem as the climax. After the loss of father, home, land, and cattle; following the loss of mother and sister; subsequent to the loss of freedom and the total rejection of all attempts to love; beyond all of this in time comes the possession of something which is all his own—though an animal—the ownership of a being he has saved and that loves him. Thus, the final indignity is to have this taken from him, to be given to a "pampered" boy.

Framing the violence, cruelty, and inhumanity of the action depicted are the stanzas of gentleness and love.

I sat at noontide in my tent,
   And looked across the Desert dun,
Beneath the cloudless firmament
   Far gleaming in the sun,
When from the bosom of the waste
A swarthy Stripling came in haste,
With foot unshod and naked limb;
And a tame springbok followed him.

With open aspect, frank yet bland,
   And with a modest mien he stood,
Caressing with a gentle hand
   That beast of gentle brood;
Then, meekly gazing in my face,

Said in the language of his race,
With smiling look yet pensive tone,
"Stranger—I'm in the world alone!" . . .

Such was Marossi's touching tale.
  Our breasts they were not made of stone;
His words, his winning looks prevail—
  We took him for "our own."
And One, with woman's gentle art,
Unlocked the fountains of his heart;
And love gushed forth—till he became
Her Child in everything but name.[14]

Judging correctly the effect it would have in 1834, Pringle placed "The Bechuana Boy" first in *African Sketches*. Yet in 1881, John Noble, giving South Africans a new edition because all English volumes published between 1828 and 1840 were out of print, in reproducing the South African poems offered a new arrangement. "The Bechuana Boy" now was moved almost to the center of the volume. In a complete edition by William Hay in 1912, the editor put this poem next to last. The lines had not been introduced at all in *Ephemerides,* 1828.

Despite the narrative, dramatic, and humanitarian impact of "The Bechuana Boy" in the 1830's, with the passing of time it has lost more than some of the other "Dark Folk" poems. For example, as a poet Pringle was operating with greater imaginative power in lines such as the following from "The Wild Bushman":

The countless springboks are my flock,
  Spread o'er the unbounded plain;
The buffalo bendeth to my yoke,
  The wild-horse to my rein;
My yoke is the quivering assagai,
  My rein the tough bow-string;
My bridle curb is a slender barb—
  Yet it quells the forest-king.

The crested adder honoureth me,
  And yields at my command
His poison-bag, like the honey bee,
  When I seize him on the sand.
Yea, even the wasting locust-swarm,

Which mighty nations dread,
To me nor terror brings nor harm—
For I make of them my bread.[15]

Usually in his writing Pringle concentrated upon the formal aspects of poem building and upon the idea he wished to express. Ordinarily both were predetermined. As with the poetry of many others of his own period of literature, one of the major weaknesses of his poetry is the slight attention given to the potentialities of words. The two stanzas from "The Wild Bushman" are an interesting exception. Here the author is going about the poet's business of presenting one thing in terms of another. To do this requires a conscious use of language. The process starts in the first line with the use of *flocks,* a word normally reserved for a context in which the animals referred to are domesticated. In that part of South Africa to which Pringle alludes, the possession of "flocks" was one of the great sources of wealth and one of the stabilizing facts of ownership and development. The flocks of the Bushmen were wild herds, and they belonged to Bushmen only in the sense that they lived by hunting the springbok and other animals that supplied food.

Because they lived exclusively as hunters and gatherers, the unusual methods employed by the Bushmen have always been of special interest. It is these methods that engage Pringle's attention in the quoted lines. Bushman weapons were light and frail, thus incapable of killing large game by force. As a substitute for force, they used poisoned weapons. For this purpose they gathered from the "crested adder" his "poison-bag," in one sense so different from the "honey-bag" of the bee, yet in another identical since it was the source of food, accounted for by an intermediate step. This step is introduced in the "buffalo . . . wild-horse . . . forest-king" passage. Bushman methods acted precisely as a "yoke . . . rein . . . curb" because the poisoned weapon merely checked, slowed up, the hunted animal. Finally the poisoned weapon brought under control and stopped (in this context meaning death) the hunted one. Pringle's making of the assagai the yoke, bow-string the rein, and barb the bridle curb is an accurate and imaginative touch. All of this is pressed into service in supplying meat, and finally the dreaded locusts are by the Bushmen made into their bread. Taken as a unit the passage accurately depicts in felicitous terms an important phase of Bushman existence.

Continuing his presentation of the native peoples, Pringle writes of the Kosa and Coranna in the same manner as he and other Scottish and English poets have depicted cherished sections of their own rural districts. The bitterness of the Pringle sonnets and longer statements concerning native life have been vanquished by a descriptive and lyric intention. With ease and naturalness the author presents place, people, and way of life. When he speaks of the "Coranna," he is not merely thinking of Hottentots in general but an independent tribe living on the banks of the Gareep, or Great Orange, River.

Fast by his wild resounding River
The listless Córan lingers ever;
Still drives his heifers forth to feed,
Soothed by the gorrah's humming reed;
A rover still unchecked will range,
As humour calls, or seasons change;
His tent of mats and leathern gear
All packed upon the patient steer.
'Mid all his wanderings hating toil,
He never tills the stubborn soil;
But on the milky dams relies,
And what spontaneous earth supplies.
Or, should long-parching droughts prevail,
And milk, and bulbs, and locusts fail,
He lays him down to sleep away
In languid trance the weary day;
Oft as he feels gaunt hunger's stound,
Still tightening famine's girdle round;
Lulled by the sound of the Gareep,
Beneath the willows murmuring deep:
Till thunder-clouds, surcharged with rain,
Pour verdure o'er the panting plain;
And call the famished Dreamer from his trance,
To feast on milk and game, and wake the moon-light dance.[16]

Unhesitating use of the proper words for the handling of his subject will be found in such a line as that in which the cattle are driven forth to pasture "Soothed by the gorrah's humming reed." That the "gorrah" is a musical instrument is established with naturalness by the context, and that it is peculiar to the

Hottentots may easily be guessed. Accurate depiction of habits is revealed in the line "As humour calls, or seasons change." The tribes moved because of a shifting food supply or merely humor, since they did not build with prohibiting permanence. Something of this impermanence is suggested in the statement that they live upon "what spontaneous earth supplies." Finally, as Pringle brings his brief account to an end, it is of some technical interest that the author, who had been writing with a four-foot line, concludes with a five- and then a six-foot line.

Following "The Coranna" immediately, "The Kosa" is quickly localized by the phrases "by Chumi's banks," "By Keisi's meads," "On Dèbe's slopes," "from Kalumna's wood." Though Pringle used *Kosa* to mean Caffer, his naming of places identifies the natives as the Xhosa tribe, the "red blanket" people. These are the "Dark Folk" of Francis Carey Slater, the Keisi his beloved Keiskama, which he insisted was the most beautiful river in South Africa. It was the stream about which Slater wrote his only novel, *The Shining River* (1925). Slater had read the Pringle poems with attention; it is thus evident that the early writer had started that which was being used a century later.

Though in "The Kosa" important tribal history had been introduced, the event is disposed of in five lines. "Makanna's Gathering," however, gives its entire attention to a single event. In the *Narrative* Pringle had devoted some ten pages to this piece of history. Here he told in some detail the story of Makanna, originally of low rank, who had become a chieftain of great power and influence as well as a person with prophetic claims. Initially a friend to the English, he had turned completely against them and announced he was called by Uhlanga, the Great Spirit, to destroy the men who had come from the sea. Though he gathered an extremely formidable and dangerous force to lead against troops at Grahamstown, he was defeated. This is an involved piece of history as told in prose, but Pringle converts the material into a lyric of forty-eight lines, of which the following are a fair representation:

> He bids me call you forth,
> Bold sons of Káhabee,
> To sweep the White Men from the earth,
> And drive them to the sea:

The sea, which heaved them up at first,
  For Amakósa's curse and bane,
Howls for the progeny she nurst,
  To swallow them again.

Hark! 'tis Uhlanga's voice
  From Debè's mountain caves!
He calls you now to make your choice—
  To conquer or be slaves:
To meet proud Amanglézi's guns,
  And fight like warrior's nobly born:
Or, like Umláo's feeble sons,
  Become the freeman's scorn.[17]

Writing here with direct simplicity, Pringle was looking more toward the literary future than the past—and this was good. With the same ease he wrote a sequel to "Makanna's Gathering," lines which he called "The Incantation." In the conflict between the English government and the native chieftains, Makanna was taken into custody and confined on Robben Island, in the mouth of Table Bay. He attempted to escape by seizing a fishing boat, but before he could reach shore he was upset and drowned. Makanna's "widowed bride," seeking vengeance, approaches *Indóda,* the Man Mountain, from which midway up gushes a stream. Here a ceremony is performed.

Standing by the dark blue water,
  Robed in panther's speckled hide,
Who is she? Jalúhsa's daughter,
  Bold Makanna's widowed bride.
Stern she stands, her left hand clasping
  By the arm her wondering child:
He, her shaggy mantle grasping,
  Gazes up with aspect wild.

Thrice in the soft fount of nursing
  With sharp steel she pierced a vein,—
Thrice the White Oppressor cursing,
  While the blood gushed forth amain,—
Wide upon the dark-blue water,
  Sprinkling thrice the crimson tide,—

Spoke Jalúhsa's high-souled daughter,
  Bold Makanna's widowed bride.

"Thus into the Demon's River
  Blood instead of milk I fling:
Hear, Uhlanga—great Life-Giver!
  Hear, Togúgh—Avenging King!
Thus the Mother's feelings tender
  In my breast I stifle now:
Thus I summon you to render
  Vengeance for the Widow's vow!" [18]

Presenting one area of feminine reaction in "The Incantation," in "The Ghona Widow's Lullaby" the author developed a very different reaction. Almost everything about the raw materials of this poem was of personal importance to Thomas Pringle. The widow around whom the poem is built belonged to the Ghonaque Hottentots, original inhabitants of the Kat River area, and one of those who in 1829 returned to this district as free people. At that time, however, it was necessary to drive out by force the Bantu chieftain, Makomo, who with his tribe occupied the territory. This explains Makomo's resentment and the danger at all times of Bantu attack upon the Hottentots. Pringle had followed in detail these events and finally recorded them in his *Narrative*.

Already it has been made clear that among the native peoples it was only the Hottentots that Pringle knew from personal experience. They became the first to whom he offered Christian training during the early months at Baviaans River. This period had run from July, 1820, to August, 1822. There was another residence of almost exactly a year before he left South Africa in April, 1826. It was at this time that he collected the specific materials which appear to have motivated the writing of "The Ghona Widow's Lullaby." A reader is directed to this information because for no other title among his South African poems did Thomas Pringle supply an epigraph. Here he has given five lines from Sicána's Hymn (later Ntsikana), considered the first Christian hymn composed and sung within the Bantu area. Ntsikana composed both the words and music. The Reverend John Knox Bokwe reports that "The words are in the original Kafir. . . . The tune, or chant, to which the Kafir words are sung, was published for the first time in the Sol-Fa notation at Lovedale in 1876, the music having been handed down only by tradition til then."[19] Pringle heard the hymn at Baviaans River in 1825, and he printed the words in the 1838 edition of his poems. The story of Ntsikana's life reveals why Pringle was easily moved to write this particular poem.

Ntsikana was the first Christian convert among the Kaffirs. He belonged to the Gaika tribe; and lived the usual boy and lad life of his people. One day a strange elderly white man arrived and pitched his tent on the banks of the Keiskama River. This was Dr. van der Kemp; and his words Ntsikana received as precious seed. When Dr. van der Kemp left, the Revd. Joseph Williams followed; and spoke the same message, from the same book; which "thing" the Kafir said haunted his very existence. Later, Ntsikana had visions and dreamed dreams; and one day (after he was married), on passing a stream, in the presence of his family, he washed the clay from his body; which had become the acknowledged sign of adopting Christianity. Next morning he was heard chanting a hymn, after which he made his first statement of the Christian religion. Then he stood forth as a preacher; drawing crowds to listen; and often exercising what he and others regarded as a prophetic gift. Subsequently the Revd. John Brownlee arrived at the Chumie, not far from where Ntsikana lived, who then arranged to move to the Mission Station; but before that could be carried out he was attacked with a very severe illness, which ended in his death. Before he died he said, addressing his children: "I am going home to my Father. Do not, after I die, go back to heathenism. I want you to go to Bulimeli, (Brownlee). Have nothing to do with heathen dances, but keep firm hold of the Word of God. I am going home to my Father, to my Master. Lay me down." So saying he passed away. This was in 1821. He was buried in the first coffin used for native burial, the stem of a large tree scooped out; and two of his own Christian converts conducted the funeral service.[20]

Prefacing his poem, Pringle quoted in the original language five lines from Ntsikana's Hymn: "Utíko umkúla gozizulína;/ Yebínza inquínquis Nosilimélè./ Umzi wakonána subiziélè,/ Umkokéli úa sikokéli tina;/ Uénza infáma zenza ga bómi." In English the lines read, "O Thou Mighty God of Heaven,/ Who whirlest round the stars—the Pleiades./ In Thy dwelling place on Thee we call,/ To be a leader and a guide to us,/ O Thou who to the blind givest light."[21] The full text of the poem is as follows:

The storm hath ceased: yet still I hear
  The distant thunder sounding,
And from the mountains, far and near,
  The headlong torrents bounding.
The jackal shrieks upon the rocks;
  The tiger-wolf is howling;
The panther round the folded flocks
  With stifled *gurr* is prowling.
But lay thee down in peace, my child;
God watcheth o'er us midst the wild.

I fear the Bushman is abroad—
  He loves the midnight thunder;
The sheeted lightning shows the road,
  That leads his feet to plunder:
I'd rather meet the hooded-snake
  Than hear his rattling quiver,
When, like an adder, through the brake,
  He glides along the river.
But, darling, hush thy heart to sleep—
The Lord our Shepherd watch doth keep.

The Kosa from Luhéri high
  Looks down upon our dwelling;
And shakes the vengeful assagai,—
  Unto his clansman telling
How he, for *us*, by grievous wrong,
  Hath lost these fertile valleys;
And boasts that now his hand is strong
  To pay the debt of malice.
But sleep, my child; a Mightier Arm
Shall shield thee (helpless one!) from harm.

The moon is up; a fleecy cloud
  O'er heaven's blue deeps is sailing;
The stream, that lately raved so loud,
  Makes now a gentle wailing.
From yonder crags, lit by the moon,
  I hear a wild voice crying:
'Tis but the harmless bear-baboon,
  Unto his mates replying.
Hush—hush thy dreams, my moaning dove,
And slumber in the arms of love!

The wolf, scared by the watch-dog's bay,
Is to the woods returning;
By his rock-fortress, far away,
The Bushman's fire is burning.
And hark! Sicána's midnight hymn,
Along the valley swelling,
Calls us to stretch the wearied limb,
While kinsmen guard our dwelling:
Though vainly watchmen wake from sleep,
'Unless the Lord the city keep.'

At dawn, we'll seek, with songs of praise,
Our food on the savannah,
As Israel sought, in ancient days,
The heaven-descended manna;
With gladness from the fertile land
The veld-kost we will gather,
A harvest planted by the hand
Of the Almighty Father—
From thraldom who redeems our race,
To plant them in their ancient place.

Then, let us calmly rest, my child;
Jehovah's arm is round us,
The God, the Father reconciled,
In heathen gloom who found us;
Who to his heart, by sorrow broke,
His wondrous WORD revealing,
Led me, a lost sheep, to the flock,
And to the Fount of Healing.
Oh may the Saviour-Shepherd lead
My darling where his lambs do feed![22]

Early in his poetic career, Thomas Pringle wrote a number of songs to be sung to ancient Scottish airs. Some of these were published in the collection of his poems which appeared in 1819, just before he left Edinburgh for the Cape. In each of these songs the author used a different formal pattern. Late in his career, he returned to the genre of the song in the composition of this lullaby. As one glances through the poem, he notes that here is a stanza unused in anything else that the author published. The mere fact of uniqueness, however, is not within itself important. What is significant is that the stanza is perfectly suited to what the author hopes to achieve, not only in the few lines of this one composition, but in the work of his life. Whether at the conscious or subconscious level is not very relevant, Pringle's ultimate goal seems to have been the union of the literary, the humanitarian, and the Christian. In the stanza employed, the first eight lines embody his narrative and the concluding couplet applies Christian doctrine to the action. Never with greater grace did he effect the union of his various materials.

Much of the success of the poem depends upon the convention of the lullaby, which allows the mother to sing of that which surrounds herself and the baby, anything which impinges upon their existences. Inherent in the convention is the acceptance of an emotional rather than a totally rational reaction to the whole situation. Pringle has strengthened almost immeasurably his potentialities by making the traditional *mother* a *widow*. Thus, the child will need special protection not only because small and weak but also because he is without a father.

Protection will be needed first from the violent storms of the region and the great wild beasts. Almost as natural as storms, in fact associated for good reason with storms, and spoken of as wild like the beasts, were the Bushmen. A third and very great danger was present in the Kosa, Bantu warriors intent upon revenge because of the loss of lands to the Hottentot tribe to which the widow belongs. In the couplet for each of these three stanzas, the mother assures the child of protection from God, greater than the storm, beast, Bushmen, or Kosa. Having reached this point, throughout the fourth stanza the author presents the baby asleep in safety and peace, surrounded by *love,* perhaps the most important of all Christian qualities.

Into the peaceful atmosphere which has become dominant, in the fifth stanza Sicána's hymn fills the valley at midnight. The baby sleeps while kinsmen watch. A night watch in this particular place at this particular time is historical fact not literary fancy. Yet in this stanza the final couplet makes a different kind of statement from previous comments. Here the mother reasons that the wakefulness of human watchmen is in vain unless all of man's affairs are placed in the hands of the "Great Watcher" over humanity. After the introduction of the hymn, the author freely introduces religious references (associated with historical ones) into the remaining stanzas. As the Children of Israel had gathered manna while in the wilderness, the Hottentots who had been settled in this area live, especially at first, on the "veld-kost," the wild roots and bulbs of the region. This was food they had not planted or tended and could be said to come from the "Almighty Father"—he was the planter. Picking up this last word, in the couplet the mother sings that this Father has redeemed her race from "thraldom," as he had the Children of Israel from bondage, and had "planted them in their ancient place." For the singer this was simple historical fact. Only the one to whom thanks should be given was debatable. This question, however, is completely resolved in the final stanza. All narrative has disappeared, and the lines become a song of praise to Jehovah, God, the Father, the Fount of Healing, the Saviour-Shepherd. It is He who found the Hottentot in the "heathen gloom" and brought him out of this darkness with "His wondrous WORD." It is He who had led the mother, lost as an individual, to the "flock." The mother's final hope is that the child will be brought to "where his lambs do feed!" Almost without necessity for remark is the fact that the lamb, sheep, shepherd imagery is appropriate to the South African situation, even as it was to ancient Israel.

With few if any reservations, this poem must have satisfied Thomas Pringle's desire to write something worthy of being remembered—especially since it used as subject matter the "Dark Folk" who had touched his deepest emotions.

IV *From Deep Within One's Being*

Slightly less than a century after the publication of "Afar in the Desert," George W. Robinson in a bibliographical study [23] of the poem estimated that no less than a million copies had been sold. Roughly half a century has elapsed since Robinson made his estimate. Looking back upon such a record, well might one suggest as a subtitle for this piece of work, "Riding About Africa, or How to Create a Best Seller." Certainly Thomas Pringle never entertained any such thoughts; yet, helped along by luck, he supplied the ingredients for success. The luck, of course, was needed before the substance of the lines could exercise its influence. "Afar in the Desart, A Reverie" was originally published in the April 1824 number of the *South African Journal,* issued May 7. It was signed "*Interior of South Africa* S.E." There were six stanzas (24, 18, 12, 14, 24, 10) totalling 102 lines. This was the second and last number of the *Journal* which Pringle and Fairbairn had started in Cape Town. Circulation was extremely limited, making it impossible for the poem to have been seen by many potential readers. It received its first significant circulation when it was picked up by George Thompson and printed as a note in *Travels in Southern Africa,* 1827. In introducing the material Thompson said, "Mr. Pringle's poem, 'Afar in the Desert' . . . expresses so well the feelings of a traveller in the wilderness, and contains such lively and appropriate sketches of African scenery, that, though somewhat long for a foot note, I gladly avail myself of the author's permission to add it to the other illustrations which he has kindly contributed to my work." [24]

Here in this footnote Samuel Taylor Coleridge saw the poem and wrote Pringle the letter which became the most famous one Thomas was ever to receive. Leitch Ritchie gives the following extract: "It is some four or five months ago since G. Thompson's 'Travels, &c., in Southern Africa,' passing its book-club course through our house, my eye by accident lighting on some verses, I much against my wont was tempted to go on, and so I first became acquainted with your '*Afar in the Desert.*' Though at that time so busy that I had not looked at any of the new books, I was taken so completely possession of, that for some days I did little else but read and recite your poem, now to this group and now to that; and since that time have either written, or caused to be written, at least half a dozen copies, and procured my friend, Mr. Gillman, who, and not I, is a member of the book-club, to purchase the two volumes for me. The day before yesterday I sent a copy in my own hand to my son, the Rev. D. Coleridge, or rather to his bride, at Helston, Cornwall, and then discovered that it had been reprinted in the *Athenaeum;* with the omission of about four, or at the utmost of six lines. I do not hesitate to declare it, among the two or three most perfect lyric poems in our language. 'Praecepitandus est liber Spiritus,' says the critic; and you have thoroughly fulfilled the prescript." [25]

Statements of this kind reveal more about the letter writer than the poem discussed. Yet Pringle had every right to feel complimented by this recognition from Coleridge. Such words give an author the courage to continue against the obstacles the world usually places before serious literary effort. Sir Walter Scott had offered the same type of encouragement to the youthful author;

now Coleridge gave his support as middle age approached. It is not to be assumed, though, that Thomas was idle in his own behalf. At the same time that he was using the lines at Cape Town he was sending them to England, where they appeared in the *Wesleyan Methodist Magazine*, February, 1825.[26] Thus the poem was published in England nine months after it was first seen in the Cape. Slightly more than two years later, May, 1827, it was offered the readers of the *Ladies' Monthly Museum*.[27] This coincided with Thompson's use of the poem in his *Travels*. The lines Coleridge had discovered in the *Athenaeum*, March, 1828, were part of a review of Pringle's 1828 collection which he called *Ephemerides*.[28] "Afar in the Desert" had naturally been included here among the South African material; in fact it was placed first. Another critic, in the *Eclectic Review*, April, 1828, printed the poem, with a comment, "We do not much like the rough gallop of the following lines, but we forgive the measure for the sake of the poetry, as we should do a jolting road leading through a beautiful country." [29]

Wide approval which develops rapidly often is focused upon a poem with an obvious sound pattern rather than a subtle one. Thus, a reader is not surprised to find that the auditory characteristics of "Afar in the Desert" are extremely simple and restricted in scope. In fact almost everything about the poem is restricted to the point that it moves in the direction of monotony. If the length had been extended to two or three hundred lines, continued reading would have become painful. Not only is the poem written in couplets, but tetrameter rather than the more flexible pentameter line. In the use of a four-beat measure, Pringle appears to have sought rather than avoided a caesural break which divided his line into balanced halves. While English poetry is naturally and normally iambic, Pringle has introduced into his lines some fifty or more percent anapaestic feet. Though the anapaest as a variant is extremely useful, the anapaest in quantity is rather certainly the most monotonous measure in English. Finally, in these lines Pringle has employed alliteration in a ratio almost comparable to Anglo-Saxon verse. With little doubt these characteristics gave him an immediate audience, but it was other qualities that held the readers.

Very deep in man is the desire to hear about that which is far away, especially if there is any suggestion of strangeness. For the most part, Pringle satisfied this desire with animal names. Few Europeans had any very clear idea of what they would be encountering if they found before them an oribi, gnu, hartebeest, kudu, or eland. Not many readers had seen a South African buffalo, perhaps not even a picture, nor would they have known a quagga. Though Pringle does little more with his animals than catalogue them, even this seems to have been satisfactory to his early audience.

Despite the interest of readers in animals, it appears to have been Pringle's presentation of the Karroo that not only attracted but held his readers. What he identifies as "the pathless depths of the parched Karroo" dominates two of the six sections of the poem. The second of these is the more effective.

> Away-away—in the Wilderness vast,
> Where the White Man's foot hath never passed,
> And the quivered Coránna or Bechuán
> Hath rarely crossed with his roving clan:
> A region of emptiness, howling and drear,
> Which Man hath abandoned from famine and fear;
> Which the snake and the lizard inhabit alone,
> With the twilight bat from the yawning stone;
> Where grass, nor herb, nor shrub takes root,
> Save poisonous thorns that pierce the foot;
> And the bitter-melon, for food and drink,
> Is the pilgrim's fare by the salt lake's brink:
> A region of drought, where no river glides,
> Nor rippling brook with osiered sides;
> Where sedgy pool, nor bubbling fount,
> Nor tree, nor cloud, nor misty mount,
> Appears, to refresh the aching eye:
> But the barren earth and the burning sky,
> And the blank horizon, round and round,
> Spread—void of living sight or sound.[30]

When Thompson said that he included in his *Travels* Pringle's "Afar in the Desert" because it "contains such lively and appropriate sketches of African scenery," he was careless in either his reading of the lines or in the composition of his comment upon the lines—or both. Specific scenic images are precluded by the general diction employed. The Great Karroo is given as a

"Wilderness vast . . . region of emptiness . . . drought . . . the barren earth and the burning sky./ And the blank horizon, round and round,/ Spread, void of living sight or sound." This is the area in its totality, not scenes somewhere in the whole. The same general approach is used when he writes that "grass, nor herb, nor shrub takes root"—not somewhere but everywhere. Even "the snake and the lizard inhabit alone" not a particular spot but the region. Using the same type of diction, he identifies what the Karroo lacks: "no river glides,/ Nor rippling brook. . . ./ Where sedgy pool, nor bubbling fount,/ Nor tree, nor cloud, nor misty mount,/ Appears. . . ." Other negatives offer this as a region over which "the White Man's foot hath never passed . . . the quivered Coránna or Bechuán/ Hath rarely crossed. . . . Which Man hath abandoned from famine and fear. . . ." Before this point has been reached, Pringle's strategy is quite clear: not only the traveler but the reader gazes into a region with horror. The intention was not to present a scene but to create an emotion, and in this the author has been successful.

If the speaker in the poem believes the desert, the Karroo, to be a place of horror, why would he or anyone else ever enter it? The answer is very definite: because a greater horror is driving him toward the lesser one, even making him welcome the lesser, the desert.

> When the wild turmoil of this wearisome life,
> With its scenes of oppression, corruption, and strife—
> The proud man's frown, and the base man's fear,—
> The scorner's laugh, and the sufferer's tear,—
> And malice, and meanness, and falsehood, and folly,
> Dispose me to musing and dark melancholy;
> When my bosom is full, and my thoughts are high,
> And my soul is sick with the bondman's sigh—
> Oh! then there is freedom, and joy, and pride,
> Afar in the Desert alone to ride!
> There is rapture to vault on the champing steed,
> And to bound away with the eagle's speed. . . .[31]

Not even Hamlet in one of his most despondent moments broods over any such list of the ills that "human flesh is heir to" as the catalogue offered by Pringle. Truly there are enough to afford a wide distribution, enabling each man to have a suitable ill accorded him, or even a personal collection. Here again, though, Pringle's intention is rather distinctly general and cumulative, not specific and restricted. During the period in which the poem was written, things were going well for Thomas and his family. He accepted, however, the prevailing idea of his time, the idea that civilization is evil. If this is true, then to seek isolation in the natural world is good. In many ways the fundamental idea being proposed is sentimental and escapist. The first section of the poem makes this attitude very clear:

When the sorrows of life the soul o'ercast,
And, sick of the Present, I cling to the Past;
When the eye is suffused with regretful tears,
From the fond recollections of former years;
And shadows of things that have long since fled
Flit over the brain, like the ghosts of the dead;
Bright visions of glory—that vanished too soon;
Day-dreams—that departed ere manhood's noon;
Attachments—by fate or by falsehood reft;
Companions of early days—lost or left;
And my Native Land—whose magical name
Thrills to the heart like electric flame;
The home of my childhood; the haunts of my prime;
All the passions and scenes of that rapturous time
When the feelings were young and the world was new,
Like the fresh bowers of Eden unfolding to view;
All—all now forsaken—forgotten—foregone!
And I—a lone exile remembered of none—
My high aims abandoned,—my good acts undone,—
Aweary of all that is under the sun,—
With that sadness of heart which no stranger may scan,
I fly to the Desert afar from man! [32]

Few passages in the whole of literature written in English display so many characteristics of Romanticism as will be found here and in the other lines of the poem. There is a severe temptation to play games with "Afar in the Desert." One game might be to undertake the location of all of the ideas and key words or phrases in one writer. Another would be to identify each characteristic in a different author. Still another would be to associate a Pringle characteristic with the author in which it is dominant.

The game could go on, and though interesting would still be a game.

All playing aside, the attitudes expressed were at the time both pervasive and deep. That large numbers of readers were attracted to the poem establishes a general acceptance of the point of view expressed; that a reader such as Coleridge was moved to extravagant claims for the poem suggests that the lines have penetrated very far into his secret places. His reaction was undoubtedly a very personal one. Lying somewhere between the often superficial reading of the masses and the intensely individual evaluation of Coleridge must exist a kind of human reception which reveals both depth and universality. If such a reader does not exist, rational explanation of the continued reaction to the poem would be impossible. Even today, those who study Pringle because of his editorial work, his prose writings, his defense of freedom of the press, his efforts to free the slave, or in any way his historical importance, all—with few exceptions—give respect to this poem. Confronted with evidence of this kind, one ponders the cause.

Beyond all questions of fad, beyond characteristics with a general appeal, beyond any changes wrought by time looms one irreducible fact: man is nonsocial as well as social. He is individual and thus nonsocial before he becomes social. Ultimately, in the mature man the two are probably far from balanced, with man the individual remaining more powerful than man the social being. Should one wonder, then, that there are times when man wishes to be alone, that though a human being he desires to avoid human beings. To this wish he may assign all kinds of explanations, none of which explain. The final fact is that he wishes moments of solitude in which to commune with his own humanity. Even Pringle's final claim is absorbed into the inclusiveness of this obsession for the individual that at times descends upon man. In closing his poem the author wrote, "As I sit apart by the desert stone . . . 'A still small voice' comes through the wild . . . Which banishes bitterness, wrath, and fear,—saying—MAN IS DISTANT, BUT GOD IS NEAR!" [33] Though the author meant in a specific orthodox sense what he said here, the impact of the lines need not be diminished by the passing of nineteenth-century orthodoxy. Major twentieth-century poets have insisted that man carries within him that which transcends the physical, call it what one wishes. It is the "still small voice" itself which is the constant, not the name by which it is called. Pringle had indeed dipped his pen in a well of universal ink.

V *"Its Memory shall in my heart remain"*

No great effort need be expended to prove that "Afar in the Desert" was an imaginative projection rather than literal transcription and that it was a composite of many experiences rather than the result of any one event focused in relation to time and place. It is evident from the images of the poem that Pringle, who had ridden hundreds of miles with the silent Bushboy alone by his side, was remembering many scenes that were not in the desert. Most of the animals he had seen were not observed in the desert areas. In fact, if one accepts the lines of the poem literally, he must reject the claim that Pringle had seen either the animals or the desert itself because he states that it is a region "Where the White Man's foot hath never passed." Actually, one of the most memorable experiences of Pringle's life in South Africa was a crossing of the Great Karroo during a very severe drougth late in the winter of 1822. The trip was made with his wife and her sister Janet, and the Pringles traveled with Jacob Maré who had with him his wife and two daughters. Here were a number of white feet, and indeed there had been hundreds of others. Even the climax of the poem offers a contradiction if one is reading literally, for it says that man is far away. Actually the speaker has a man beside him. Ultimately a reader has to accept the poem as a multioriented composition. This does not indicate that the writing is either good or bad. It merely helps a reader in his approach.

Having survived a crossing of the Great Karroo while it glared from its sun-burned wastes, Pringle carried with him the images into Cape Town and made them the most effective part of his best known poem. In Cape Town and from Cape Town the poem was published. This also was the scene of his violent conflict with the governor. Upon his entrance into Cape Town, he had brought with him one poem; upon his departure, he unexpectedly found another. An accident had brought him for two months into the hands of the brothers at the Moravian Mission of Genadendal. While there he wrote, November, 1824, about them and for them a sonnet, one of the most direct statements ever to be spread on paper by the pen of Thomas Pringle. As an introduction he explains that when he lived in Scotland he had often longed to see "This quiet Vale of Grace," the meaning of the name Genadendal. Now he has been permitted to see the place in all its physical and spiritual actuality. It has been his privilege "To hear the hymns of solemn melody/ Rising from the sequestered burial ground;/ To see the heathen taught, the lost sheep found,/ The blind restored, the long-oppressed set free." [34] Having witnessed all of this, he now testifies that "Its memory shall in my heart remain;/ But yet more close familiar ties there be/ That bind me to this spot with grateful chain—/ For it hath been a Sabbath Home to me,/ Through lingering months of solitude and pain." [35] In these simple lines a reader discovers one of the reasons for Thomas Pringle's achievements. Within himself he carried that which would allow him to accept most people, places, and situations for what they were. A short time before he wrote these lines, he felt that he had been grievously wronged. For what had been done to him he hated Lord Charles Somerset, with an unreasoning hate. Yet he did not allow this emotion to transfer itself to other people. The men at Genadendal he viewed with an unforgetting love. He recoiled with horror from what many of the Boers had done to the Hottentots, but he found among the Boers many good friends and generous neighbors. Baviaans River valley he would always cherish—along with other areas of the Cape. While he deplored many of the conditions that he found in South Africa, he accepted other situations because he felt that changes that would lead to improvement were being made. Some government officials he despised, but not government itself. Thus, as he moved about this strange country, he found so much to embrace that he was never without materials for his writing. Then, the fact of final importance was that he accepted his materials in such a natural way that he did not even tell himself it was wise to accept his new environment. In truth it had become a part of him.

CHAPTER 11

Results of a Residence

THERE is a significant difference between the title used by other early writers on South Africa and the name employed by Thomas Pringle when he published the great narrative which recorded his life at the Cape. Other authors offered titles such as "Adventures and Travels," "Account of Travels," "Researches," and merely "Four Years" in the country. Pringle related himself to South Africa through the word "Residence," indicating that he *lived* there. The country belonged to him, and likewise he belonged to the country. Though he never rejected Scotland, he was able to embrace South Africa. It, too, was his land. The attitude became the foundation upon which achievement was built, and this achievement is the reason why he is worthy of study now a hundred and fifty years after he approached the Cape with serious hope. Though his hope seems to have been very considerable, his actual achievements certainly exceeded his visions.

Because in Scotland his family was losing its cherished unity and independence, he hoped in South Africa to unite Robert Pringle with his children and allow them to secure their economic independence. Despite the brevity of his own life, he lived long enough to know that his and their efforts in South Africa had met with success and that even from the early years they were able to give something to the country from which they were receiving so much. Looking back, it is possible to say that various things in South Africa are different now because this particular family emigrated in 1820. Something of the contribution of Robert Pringle's descendants has been delineated in a volume called *Pringles of the Valleys* (1957), by three twentieth century representatives of the family—Eric, Mark, and John. Starting, except for Thomas, as farmers, wool producers, and millers, the Pringles quickly made for themselves a place in the Cape. One of the contributions that would have pleased Thomas is that his family was important in the development of the Presbyterian church in South Africa. Having reached Baviaans River June 29, the Pringles observed their first Sunday, July 2, with formal worship. It was agreed that they would continue conducting services for themselves until an ordained minister could be provided. This occurred in 1828. In the same year John Pringle had started his home over the mountains from Glen-Lynden at a location to become Glen Thorn, and he erected in 1840 a building for the Presbyterian church which developed there.

Included in *Pringles of the Valleys* is a full account of the Glen Thorn church, written by the Reverend John Black, yet detailed to a point that makes brief quotation ineffective. In the same volume, however, a long excerpt from the *Reminiscences* of Robert Pears Pringle, son of John, offers a focusing statement. Born in 1829, Robert Pears recorded his memories when he was ninety.

> . . . Be it to John Pringle's lasting credit that he had not settled long on Glen Thorn, and before he had built his second and more substantial home, he erected a house for the worship of God, which still stands as a memorial to its builder. Having completed the church, the next step was to find some person or persons to conduct the services. Mr. Pringle visited the missionaries in Kaffirland, and succeeded in arranging for a quarterly service to be conducted by these pioneers of the gospel. . . . This arrangement held good for some years, until John Pringle succeeded in obtaining both a minister and a teacher from Scotland. The minister, Mr. Hepburn, did not stay for long, but ultimately made his way to Grahamstown and joined the Wesleyan Church. The teacher, Mr. Withers, on the other hand, settled down to his duties of teaching during the week, and conducting public worship on Sundays. At the close of his six years' engagement, a Kaffir war having broken out, he left and settled at Somerset East. . . . On his departure the earlier arrangements were resorted to, and a quarterly service was continued till about 1870 when a minister and missionary was found for Glen Thorn in the person of the Rev. R. S. Leslie. From that date to the present Glen Thorn has not for any lengthy period of time been without its minister. . . .
>
> To close this series of facts and reminiscences let us try to imagine what this 1820 settlement in the Adelaide and Bedford district has meant to the Empire. How well the farms have been developed! How nobly the sons of the pioneers have responded to the call of their country, be it a Kaffir war or a European conflagration! How interest-

ing if one could only indicate how many grandsons and great-grandsons have served in the European war! . . .

Surely it is good to look back and see what has been done, and, taking courage, go forward to the things that await.[1]

Even more succinct than this account is the notice that appeared in the *Graham's Town Journal,* April 7, 1864, upon the death of John Pringle, Robert Pears Pringle's father, and "the last surviving full brother of Pringle the Poet." The *Journal* commented that "Few persons among the emigrants of 1820 were better known in this Province than John Pringle, or more deservedly respected. As a thoroughly trained agriculturist he set a bright example of intelligence, industry and perseverance, the result being the creation of an establishment which was the admiration of all who visited it." [2]

Though the Pringles today have every reason to feel great satisfaction in all they have contributed to the building of South Africa, it is clear that they do not forget Thomas. On the dust jacket of *Pringles of the Valleys,* Eric, Mark, and John speak of their literary ancestor as "probably the best known Pringle of all time." They have traced the family through eight centuries in some detail and without a break; thus, their claim for Thomas carries very considerable significance. Beyond his fight for freedom of the press, his contribution to the improvement in the position of the native peoples, and all that he did to give his family a foundation upon which to begin a new existence, he gave South Africa that upon which a literature could be created.

There is no reason to believe Thomas Pringle was not honest with himself as well as with his friends and readers when he identified himself as a minor poet. Yet he longed for some assurance that he was at least that much, that when life was over he would not be forgotten as a writer. Pringle was indeed what is usually called a minor poet. With almost no exceptions, he used the poetic tradition he inherited. That the materials he found in the Cape did not fit into the forms he brought with him seems never to have been completely understood. The one really useful influence appears to have been Wordsworth, who directed him toward greater simplicity. Most of the conscious aspects of Pringle's literary mind were liabilities. Yet from the subconscious gradually emerged two assets. Not because of his poetic theories but by his deepest beliefs Pringle was directed to his raw materials. Tenaciously held beliefs moved him to visit mission stations and prompted him to take careful note of native peoples. Natural curiosity directed his investigation of the physical world through which he moved. What is important here is not his attitudes but the fact that these materials represented the objective existence of the country. By example he indicated to future generations that they should use the substance that was uniquely their own. Those who followed were slow to comprehend the meaning. Yet only the writers who accepted advice implicit in Pringle's work achieved any success. Finally one arrived who said, "I am a South African!" His claim was quite literally true, and he was the first to create a sufficient body of writing on purely South African subjects to become an influence. After him a significant literary tradition emerged.

Before Thomas Pringle first gazed across the Cape flats from the deck of the *Brilliant*, he had commenced the study of what is now known as Afrikaans. Obviously, the language would be of practical value to him in his dealings with the Boers and the Hottentots, in fact, with all of the Dutch population and most of the servant class of the country. It has already been noted that even on the first night out on the way to Baviaans River Thomas was observing the native languages. Approaching the language situation in this extremely natural way, Pringle displayed no self-consciousness when he began to use in his poems words that belonged to the world in which he now lived and about which he was writing. Thus from the very first, he shows no hesitancy in the use of South African words. Here again Pringle showed the way for those who were to come. Francis Carey Slater had spoken Xhosa from his childhood; and when he started to write the "Dark Folk" series, he considered composing in the Xhosa language and then making English translations. Slater had also spoken Afrikaans from youth, and it is perhaps worthy of mention that the most ambitious book of his career is a presentation of the Great Trek—Afrikaans, not English, history. Slater was distinctly English. Then, into the twentieth century, one finds Roy Campbell speaking Zulu as well as writing about the Zulus. Slater and Campbell are representative rather than isolated examples revealing the direction taken by South African poetry.

Though Pringle wished to be remembered as a poet and though

he would be pleased to find what an important position his poems have taken in South African literature, he would be surprised to find that, with few exception, readers, scholars, and critics select the *Narrative of a Residence in South Africa* as the great work of his life. Here in his prose, the twentieth century, and especially the reader outside South Africa, finds Pringle controlling his medium rather than allowing the medium to control him. In fact, when Pringle is at his best, the reader forgets that there is a medium of transmission and is unconcerned with whether or not the author was aware of his technique. South Africa spreads before him and alone demands attention. When the book is finally closed, the reader knows that for several hundred pages he has been a resident of the Cape.

Spirit of Thomas Pringle, view the scenes and events in your *Narrative!* How could you fail to know that in this book your genius was employed? "*I knew, I knew. At times my fingers trembled as I saw the lines written in my journal. Years later, in London, as I prepared pages for the printer, the city disappeared from around me, and I saw on the left a strange wild coast beyond the deck of the* BRILLIANT. *The scene faded into soil that stretched beneath the heat of a burning sun. Suddenly there was a thundering noise as if a storm had broken upon us. It was a lion. A person entered the room, and London was around me again. Yes, I know something of the results of a residence.*"

Notes and References

Chapter One

1. Fairbairn Papers, No. 56, South Africa, Library of Parliament. From Graaff-Reinet, August 5, 1825.
2. *Ibid.*
3. *The Poetical Works of Thomas Pringle,* with a Sketch of His Life by Leitch Ritchie (London, 1838). "Memoirs of Thomas Pringle," Leitch Ritchie, p. cxl.
4. Thomas Pringle, *Narrative of a Residence in South Africa,* introduction, biographical and historical notes by A. M. Lewin Robinson (Cape Town, 1966). "A Biographical Sketch," Josiah Conder (1835), p. xxii. Also Eric, Mark, and John Pringle, *Pringles of the Valleys* (Adelaide, C.P., South Africa, 1957), pp. 11–13.
5. Conder, "Biographical Sketch," pp. xxi–xxiii.
6. Jane Meiring, *Thomas Pringle, His Life and Times* (Cape Town and Amsterdam, 1968), p. 15.
7. Conder, "Biographical Sketch," p. xxvii (Note).
8. Meiring, pp. 17–18.
9. Ritchie, "Memoirs," p. xxxvii.
10. "Letters of Thomas Pringle to Sir Walter Scott," A. M. L. R[obinson], *Quarterly Bulletin of the South African Library,* 6(2) (1951), p. 51.
11. Meiring, p. 20.
12. *Narrative,* p. 2.

Chapter Two

1. *Narrative,* p. 2.
2. *Ibid.,* pp. 6–7.
3. *Ibid.,* p. 33.
4. *Ibid.*
5. *The South African Journal,* Vol. I, No. 1 (1824), pp. 26–33, and No. 2, pp. 118–25 and p. 126.
6. *Narrative,* p. 48.
7. *Ibid.,* pp. 77–82.

8. *Ibid.*, p. 105.
9. *Ibid.*, p. 120.

Chapter Three

1. *Narrative*, p. 174.
2. *Ibid.*, p. 180.
3. Meiring, p. 4.
4. *Ibid.*
5. *Narrative*, pp. 188–90.
6. A. M. Lewin Robinson, *None Daring to Make Us Afraid* (Cape Town, 1962), pp. 33–34.
7. Meiring, p. 100.

Chapter Four

1. *South African Journal*, Vol. I, No. 1 (1824), p. 33.
2. *Ibid.*, p. 8.
3. *Ibid.*, p. 9.
4. *Ibid.*
5. *Ibid.*, p. 24.
6. *Ibid.*
7. *Ibid.*, pp. 24–25.
8. *Ibid.*, p. 25.
9. *South African Journal*, Vol. I, No. 2 (1824), p. 105.
10. *Narrative*, p. 13.
11. *Ibid.*, p. 51.
12. *Ibid.*, p. 77.
13. *Ibid.*, p. 89.
14. *South African Journal*, Vol. I, No. 2, pp. 106–7.
15. *Ibid.*, p. 126.
16. *Ibid.*, p. 125.
17. *South African Journal*, Vol. I. No. 1, pp. 17–21.
18. *Ibid.*, p. 28.
19. *Ibid.*, pp. 32–33.
20. *South African Journal*, Vol. I. No. 2, p. 118.
21. *Ibid.*, p. 120.
22. *Ibid.*, pp. 123–24.
23. *Ibid.*, p. 125.
24. *Ibid.*, p. 151.
25. *Ibid.*, pp. 153–54.

Chapter Five

1. Thomas Pringle, *Some Account of the Present State of the English Settlers in Albany, South Africa* (London and Edinburgh, 1824), pp. iii-iv.
2. *Ibid.*, pp. 4–5.
3. *Ibid.*, pp. 5–7.
4. *Ibid.*, p. 11.
5. *Ibid.*, pp. 32–34.
6. *Ibid.*, pp. 34–37.
7. *Ibid.*, pp. 41–42. Note.

Chapter Six

1. Meiring, pp. 106–9.
2. Fairbairn Papers, No. 46. From Baviaans River, May 13, 1825.
3. Meiring, p. 7.
4. Thomas Pringle, *Ephemerides; or, Occasional Poems, written in Scotland and South Africa* (London, 1828), p. 3.
5. *Ibid.*, pp. 12–13.
6. In the order given, quoted from Oliver Goldsmith, Thomas Gray, Edward Young, James Thomson, Joseph Wharton, and George Crabbe.
7. *Ephemerides*, pp. 24–26.
8. *Ibid.*, pp. 11–12.
9. *Ibid.*, p. 53.
10. *Ibid.*
11. *Ibid.*, p. 55.
12. *Ibid.*, p. 58.
13. *Ibid.*, p. 62.
14. *Ibid.*, p. 63.
15. *Ibid.*, p. 67.
16. *Ibid.*, pp. 69–70.
17. *Ibid.*, p. 73.
18. *Poetical Works*, pp. 159–60.
19. *Ephemerides*, p. 23.
20. *Ibid.*, p. 24.
21. *Ibid.*, p 52.
22. *Ibid.*, p. 42.
23. *Ibid.*, p. 46.
24. *Ibid.*, pp. 104–5.
25. *Ibid.*, pp. 112–14.
26. *Ibid.*, p. 144.
27. *Ibid.*, p. 145.
28. *Ibid.*, p. 146.
29. *Ibid.*, p. 143.

30. *Ibid.*, p. 151.
31. *Ibid.*
32. *Ibid.*, p. 147.
33. *Ibid.*, p. 156.
34. *Ibid.*, p. 148.
35. *Ibid.*, p. 155.
36. *New Centenary Book of South Africa Verse*, ed. Francis Carey Slater (London, New York, Toronto, 1945), pp. 12–13.
37. Campbell, in explanation of Adamastor, says: "The spirit of the Cape whose apparition and prophecy form one of the finest passages in *The Lusiads* of Camoëns."
38. *The Collected Poems of Roy Campbell* (London, 1955), p. 27.

Chapter Seven

1. Meiring, p. 159.
2. *Ibid.*, p. 136.
3. Fairbairn Papers. From London, November 23, 1829. Quoted from Meiring, p. 137.
4. Meiring, p. 149.
5. Thomas Carlyle, *The Life of John Sterling* (London, 1888), p. 46.
6. Ritchie, "Memoirs," xcvii-xcviii.
7. Meiring, p. 137.
8. Fairbairn Papers, No. 52, A & B. From Baviaans River, June 29, 1825.
9. Fairbairn Papers, No. 52B. From Baviaans River, June 29, 1825.
10. Fairbairn Papers, No. 56D. From Graaff-Reinet, August 5, 1825.
11. Meiring, p. 117.
12. *Ibid.*
13. *Narrative*, p. 228.
14. *Ibid.*, pp. 228–29.
15. Meiring, p. 144.
16. Fairbairn Papers, No. 148. From London, November 1833.

Chapter Eight

1. Fairbairn Papers, No. 150. From London, May 22, 1834.
2. Fairbairn Papers, No. 150A-B-C. From London, May 22, 1834.
3. *Narrative*, p. 7.
4. *Ibid.*, pp. 8–9.
5. *Ibid.*, pp. 87–88.
6. *Ibid.*, pp. 53–55.
7. *Ibid.*, p. 316.
8. *Ibid.*, p. 319.

9. *Ibid.*, p. 224.
10. *Ibid.*
11. *Ibid.*, pp. 224–25.
12. I. Schapera, *The Koisan Peoples of South Africa* (London, 1951), pp. 29–30.
13. *Ibid.*, p. 41.
14. *Ibid.*, p. 43.
15. *Narrative*, p. 241.
16. *Ibid.*, p. 250.
17. *Ibid.*, p. 251.
18. *Ibid.*, p. 252.
19. *Ibid.*
20. *Ibid.*, pp. 257–58.
21. *Ibid.*, p. 265
22. *Ibid.*, p. 321.
23. *Ibid.*, pp. 23–24.
24. *Ibid.*, pp. 25–26.
25. *Ibid.*, p. 160.

Chapter Nine

1. Ritchie, "Memoirs," p. cxlii.
2. *Quarterly Review*, No. CIX (December, 1835), pp. 74–75.
3. Ritchie, "Memoirs," p. cxxx.
4. Conder, "Biographical Sketch," p. xxi.
5. Ritchie, "Memoirs," p. x.
6. *Ibid.*, pp. cxxxi–cxxxiii.
7. Conder, "Biographical Sketch," p. xxv.

Chapter Ten

1. Fairbairn Papers, Nos. 150 and 150A. From London, May 22, 1834.
2. *Poetical Works*, p. 25.
3. *Ibid.*, p. 28.
4. *Ibid.*, pp. 29–30.
5. *Ibid.*, p. 31.
6. *Ephemerides*, p. 202.
7. *Narrative*, p. 12.
8. *Poetical Works*, p. 33.
9. Thomas Pringle, *African Sketches* (London, 1834), p. 501.
10. Fairbairn Papers. From Eildon, October 12, 1825.
11. *Poetical Works*, p. 7.
12. *Ibid.*, p. 5.
13. *Ibid.*, pp. 4–6.

14. *Ibid.*, pp. 3–8.
15. *Ibid.*, pp. 11–12.
16. *Ibid.*, pp. 12–13.
17. *Ibid.*, p. 34.
18. *Ibid.*, pp. 36–37.
19. *Thomas Pringle: His Life, Times, and Poems,* Edited by William Hay (Cape Town, 1912), pp. 254–55.
20. *Ibid.*, p. 254.
21. *Ibid.*, p. 212.
22. *Poetical Works,* pp. 50–52.
23. George W. Robinson, *Papers of the Bibliographical Society of America,* 1923, V. 17 (1), pp. 21–54.
24. *Ibid.*, p. 33. Printed as a footnote on pp. 233–36 of *Travels in Southern Africa,* by George Thompson (London: Henry Colburn, 1827).
25. Ritchie, "Memoirs," p. cxlii.
26. *Papers of the Bibliographical Society,* p. 39.
27. *Ibid.*
28. *Ibid.*
29. *Ibid.*, p. 40.
30. *Poetical Works,* pp. 10–11.
31. *Ibid.*, p. 9.
32. *Ibid.*, pp. 8–9.
33. *Ibid.*, p. 11.
34. *Ibid.*, p. 67.
35. *Ibid.*

Chapter Eleven

1. *Pringles of the Valleys,* pp. 116–17.
2. Eric Pringle, *These Are My People* (Adelaide, C.P.), p. 19.

Selected Bibliography

PRIMARY SOURCES
(Chronological Order)

The Autumnal Excursion, or Sketches in Teviotdale; with Other Poems. Edinburgh: Constable, 1819.

Some Account of the Present State of the English Settlers in Albany, South Africa. London and Edinburgh: Underwood, 1824.

Ephemerides; or Occasional Poems, written in Scotland and South Africa. London: Smith, Elder, 1828.

Glen-Lynden: A Tale of Teviotdale. London: Smith, Elder, 1828. A copy is owned by the South African Library, the booklet at some time having been bound with *Ephemerides,* both inscribed by the author to Lt. Col. C. R. Fox. In the binding process, one margin of *Glen-Lynden* was trimmed. A short preface, dated July 19, 1828, indicates that Pringle wrote the fragment at Genadendal, November, 1824. He had intended to develop the forty-two Spenserian stanzas into a long narrative poem. Significant expansion seems never to have been effected, though at some period the author developed stanza 26 into three stanzas. The three stanzas following the ballad "Our native Land–our native Vale" were shifted to serve as an introduction. In this form the fragment, entitled "The Emigrants," seems to have been unused until it appeared in John Noble's edition of 1881 (pages 3–27) and William Hay's edition of 1912 (pages 175–190).

African Sketches. London: Moxon, 1834. Part One: Poems Illustrative of South Africa. Part Two: Narrative of a Residence in South Africa.

Narrative of a Residence in South Africa. London: Moxon, 1835. A new edition of the second part of *African Sketches* (1834), to which is prefixed a biographical sketch of the author, by Josiah Conder.

Südafrikanische Skizzen. Stuttgart und Tubingen: Cotta, 1836. First translation into another language of *Narrative of a Residence in South Africa.*

Narrative of a Residence in South Africa, und den neuester Berichten deutscher Ansiedler in der Capcolonie bearbeitet von Dr. F. H. Ungewitter: neu illustrirte Ausgabe. Leipzig: Goedsche, 183–.

Schetsen en Tafereelen uit Zuid-Afrika. Groningen: van Boekeren, 1837.

The Poetical Works of Thomas Pringle, with a Sketch of His Life by Leitch Ritchie. London: Moxon, 1838. The volume has two title pages. The first, with a signed portrait, left, of Thomas Pringle and an illustrative engraving, dates the publication 1837. The second title page is in some copies dated 1838 and in others 1839. The "Advertisement" page saying "This work is not published in the usual way, but entirely for the benefit of Mr. Pringle's Widow" is dated January 6, 1838.

Narrative of a Residence in South Africa. London: Moxon, 1840. A new edition, with double-columned pages.

Narrative of a Residence in South Africa (in *Voyages and Travels*). London: Moxon, 1842. Without the original title page.

Narrative of a Residence in South Africa (in *Smith's Standard Library*). William Smith, 1844. With the Moxon title page following the Smith wrapper.

Narrative of a Residence in South Africa. London: Tegg, 1851.

Afar in the Desert: and other South African Poems, with a Memoir and Notes, edited by John Noble. London and Cape Town, 1881. Memoir of thirty-four pages but with little new material.

South African Sketches: Poems by Thomas Pringle. Edinburgh: Abbey Press, 1902. This volume brought Pringle into the twentieth century.

Thomas Pringle: His Life, Times, and Poems, edited by William Hay. Cape Town: Juta, 1912. Biographical sketch of fifty-four pages following Conder, Ritchie, the *Narrative,* and a few later writers, such as Meurant.

Narrative of a Residence in South Africa, with introduction, biographical and historical notes by A. M. Lewin Robinson. Cape Town: Struik, 1966. This volume gives the biographical sketch by Josiah Conder, published with the edition of 1835. The notes offer full coverage but are concise–as well as clear and dependable.

Thomas Pringle in South Africa, 1820–1826, Edited with an Introduction and Notes by John Robert Wahl. Cape Town: Longman, 1970. There are eleven large color plates and eight line drawings.

Poems Illustrative of South Africa, African Sketches: Part One, Edited with an Introduction and Notes by John Robert Wahl. Cape Town: Struik, 1970. An appropriate publication upon the hundred and fiftieth anniversary of the landing of Thomas Pringle in South Africa. This is a handsome limited edition of his South African poems.

Letters, from the Fairbairn Papers, Library of Parliament, South Africa. Unpublished.

Anthologies (Chronological Order)

Albyn's Anthology (1816–1818), edited by Alexander Campbell. Vol. I: "The Banks of Cayle," pp. 36–37; "I'll Bid my Heart Be Still," pp. 40–41. Vol. II: "A Love Song" ("The Dark-Haired Maid"), pp. 10–11; "Mary of Glenfyne," pp. 50–51.

Friendship's Offering. While Pringle was editor, 1828–35, inclusive, each volume contained something of his own.

Poetry of the Cape of Good Hope, selected from the Periodical Journals of the Colony, by R. J. Stapleton. Cape Town: Greig, 1828. George W. Robinson did not mention this in his bibliography of "Afar in the Desert."

Klass Gezwint en zijn Paert: and other songs and rijmpies of South Africa. Cape Town: Juta, 1884.

The Poetry of South Africa, collected and arranged by Alexander Wilmot. London: Sampson Low; Cape Town: Juta, 1887. Represents the first half century as Francis Carey Slater's anthology offered the first full century of South African Verse. Concerning Count Wilmot's collection, Slater commented that the bulk of the South African poems by Pringle were used, along with the work of the first South African-born poet, William Rodger Thomson. Except for Pringle and several individual poems, Slater considered little else of value.

A Treasury of South African Poetry and Verse, collected from various sources and arranged by Edward Heath Crouch. London: Walter Scott; Cape Town: Juta, 1907. There was a second edition in 1909. In various ways Crouch's anthology shows an advance over Wilmot.

Sonnets of South Africa, selected by Edward Heath Crouch. London: Fifield, 1911.

Gold Dust: Siftings from South African Poems which most closely reflect the Life, Scenery, Fauna, and Flora of South Africa, selected by Edward Heath Crouch. London: Fifield, 1917.

The Centenary Book of South African Verse, 1820–1925, chosen and arranged by Francis Carey Slater. London: Longmans, Green,

1925. In a volume of two hundred and twenty pages which presents sixty-eight authors, the editor gave Pringle ten pages.

The New Centenary Book of South African Verse, chosen and arranged by Francis Carey Slater. London: Longmans, Green, 1945. Changes in the selection displayed Pringle to a better advantage.

South African Poetry, edited by Roy Macnab and Charles Gulston. London: Collins, 1949.

A Book of South African Verse, selected and introduced by Guy Butler. London and Cape Town: Oxford, 1959. Butler does his very best to ignore Pringle.

Periodicals (Chronological Order)

Poetic Mirror, edited by James Hogg, 1816. "Epistle to Mr. R. S." Pringle dates this poem from Edinburgh, 1811. Greatly expanded, it became his first major poem, "An Autumnal Excursion." It was addressed to his close friend Robert Story. In 1816, identifying it as an imitation of Sir Walter Scott, Pringle sent the poem to Scott, who commented that he wished his own notes on the subject "had always been as fine as their echo."

Edinburgh Monthly Magazine (later *Blackwood's Edinburgh Magazine*), when Pringle was editor. During this period (April-September 1817) the magazine contained the following by Pringle: "Notices concerning the Scottish Gypsies" (notes for which were said to have been supplied by Scott), April, May, September, pp. 43–58, pp. 154–61, pp. 615–20; "The Wreath," June, p. 277; "Song—Maid of my heart—a long farewell," June, p. 277; two sonnets—"To a young Lady caressing her Infant Brother" and "To a revered Female Relative," August, p. 502.

Constable's *Edinburgh Magazine and Literary Miscellany,* 1817–1818. While Pringle was editor, the magazine contained the following of his work: "Border Sketches," August, 1817, p. 43, and October, 1817, pp. 236–39; "The Minstrel's Vision, or, The Isle of Eyra," August, 1817, p. 63; "Streams, whose torrent waters glide," September, 1817, p. 162; two songs (later published in the second volume of *Albyn's Anthology*), October, 1817, p. 263ff.; "To a Lady, inclosing some MS Poems," March, 1818, p. 267; "The Legend of the Rose," June, 1818, p. 566; "Of love, and love's delight no more I sing," June, 1818, p. 566.

The South African Journal, Vol. I, No. 1, January-February, 1824. "Verses, On seeing in a late packet of English Papers, the Surrender of Cadiz, and the Proscription of a Free Press in Germany and Switzerland,—by Order of the 'Holy Alliance,'" pp. 8–9;

"Description of the Zureveld," pp. 17–21; "An Emigrant's Song," p. 24; "Sonnet, Written on a Visit to the Moravian Missionary Institution of Enon, or White Water, South Africa," p. 25; "Caffer Song," p. 25; "On the Character and Habits of Some of the Wild Animals of South Africa, No. 1, The Lion," pp. 26–33; "Wedded Love," p. 33. Vol. I, No. 2, March-April, 1824. "Afar in the Desart, A Reverie," pp. 105–7; "On the Character and Habits of Some of the Wild Animals of South Africa, No. 2, The Lion," pp. 118–25; "The Lion and the Camelopard," p. 126; "On the Present State and Prospects of the English Emigrants in South Africa," pp. 151–60.

Wesleyan Methodist Magazine, February, 1825, p. 143ff. The first appearance in England of "Afar in the Desert."

New Monthly Magazine, "Letters from South Africa." Dated Cape of Good Hope, Jan. 5, 1826, and signed "Y," "Slavery," XVII (1826), pp. 481–88. "Caffer Campaigns,–The Prophet Makanna," XIX (1827), pp. 69–76. "Government of Lord Charles Somerset. Prize Negroes at the Cape," XX (1827), pp. 209–14. "The British Government at the Cape of Good Hope. Treatment of the Natives," XXII (1828), pp. 165–72.

The Winter's Wreath (London, 1828). "Scenes in South Africa. Franschehoek," pp. 301–7.

The Iris: A Literary and Religious Offering, edited by Rev. Thomas Dale (London, 1930). "The Slave Dealer," pp. 129–31. (Also in *African Sketches*, pp. 91–93 and *Poetical Works*, pp. 58–59.)

The New Year's Gift and Juvenile Souvenir, edited by Mrs. Alaric Watts (London, 1830). "The African Mier-Vark," pp. 80–83.

The Remembrance, edited by Thomas Roscoe (London, 1831). "Pangola, an African Tale," pp. 169–80.

SECONDARY SOURCES

1. Books

MEIRING, JANE. *Thomas Pringle: His Life and Times*. Cape Town and Amsterdam: Balkema, 1968. The first attempt to present the life of Thomas Pringle with the addition of any quantity of new material since Josiah Conder (1835) and Leitch Ritchie (1838), close personal friends, wrote biographical sketches as introductions, Conder to the *Narrative* and Ritchie the *Poetical Works*. It is significant that the first effort to write a biography of Pringle has come from South Africa.

MEURANT, L. H. *Sixty Years Ago*. Cape Town: Africana Connoisseurs Press, 1963. Facsimile Reproduction of *Sixty Years Ago; or,*

Reminiscences of the Struggle for the Freedom of the Press in South Africa, and the Establishment of the First Newspaper in the Eastern Province, by The Honorable L. H. Meurant. Cape Town: Solomon, 1885. The author was involved in the struggle for freedom of the press but reports on the events long after the fight was won.

ROBINSON, A. M. LEWIN. *None Daring To Make Us Afraid*, A Study of English Periodical Literature in the Cape Colony from its beginning in 1824 to 1835. Cape Town: Miller, 1962. Careful and knowledgeable scholarship has created a study which can be used with confidence.

PRINGLE, ERIC, MARK, and JOHN. *Pringles of the Valleys, Their History and Genealogy*. Adelaide, Cape Province, South Africa, 1957. The beauty of this volume makes it a joy to use, and there is no substitute for genealogy when needed.

2. Material in Books.

LEISHMAN, JAMES FLEMING. *A Son of Knox and other Studies*. Glasgow, 1909. Pp. 41–62. One of the essays that helped bring Pringle into the twentieth century.

McLEOD, A. L. *The Commonwealth Pen: An Introduction to the Literature of the British Commonwealth*, Ithaca, New York: Cornell, 1961. P. 79. A just appraisal of Pringle's work, though short.

MILLER, G. W., and SERGEANT, HOWARD. *A Critical Survey of South African Poetry in English*. Cape Town and Amsterdam: Balkema, 1957. Chapter 2, "Thomas Pringle, the Forerunner," pp. 14–26. Informative, carefully developed, and sensible in its conclusions.

REDDING, CYRUS. *Fifty Years' Recollections*. London, 1858. (3 Vols.) II, p. 223ff., p. 227, and III, pp. 7–9. There is a letter from Pringle to Redding.

3. Material in Periodicals

CLARK, JOHN. "A Study of Pringle," *The South African Quarterly* (March 1921), pp. 10–14 (June, 1921), pp. 8–11.

R[OBINSON], A. M. L. "Thomas Pringle and Sir Walter Scott," *Quarterly Bulletin of the South African Library*, Vol. VI (2), 1951, pp. 50–56.

———. "Thomas Pringle and Sir Walter Scott," *Quarterly Bulletin of the South African Library*, Vol. VI (4), 1952, pp. 109–17.

———. "A Letter from Thomas Pringle to Sir George Mackenzie," *Quarterly Bulletin of the South African Library*, Vol. VII (2), 1952, pp. 48–51.

———. "Coleridge Advises Thomas Pringle," *Quarterly Bulletin of the South African Library,* Vol. XXIII (3), 1969, pp. 68–79.

ROBINSON, GEORGE W. "A Bibliography of Thomas Pringle's 'Afar in the Desert,'" *Papers of the Bibliographical Society of America,* Vol. XVII, Part I, 1923, pp. 21–54. This is by far the most complete and scholarly study made of any of the work of Thomas Pringle during the first hundred years following his arrival at the Cape. As an addendum to Robinson should be noted Maurice Green, "Thomas Pringle's 'Afar in the Desert,'" *Quarterly Bulletin of the South African Library,* Vol. II (4), 1948, pp. 110–12.

4. Monographs

ARMSTRONG, GEORGE. *Thomas Pringle.* Durban/Pietermaritzburg: University of Natal Library, 1964. A lecture delivered by a Cradock businessman, in 1886, and repeated in 1887 by request. The importance of the performance (since there is no new material in the paper) is that it demonstrates that Pringle's name was being kept alive in South Africa, even in the villages.

PRINGLE, ERIC. *These Are My People.* Adelaide, Cape Province, South Africa: Privately produced, 1967. A thirty-page story of the Pringles, in both English and Afrikaans. There are details here unavailable elsewhere.

5. Reviews

Athenaeum, March 14, 1828. Review of *Ephemerides.*

Cape of Good Hope Literary Gazette, Vol. IV, No. 12, 1834. Review of *African Sketches.*

Eclectic Review, May, 1820, pp. 481–84. Review of *Autumnal Excursion.*

Eclectic Review, June, 1824, pp. 571–74. Review of *Some Account of the Present State of the British Settlers in Albany, South Africa.*

Eclectic Review, April, 1828. A review of *Ephemerides.*

Edinburgh Magazine and Literary Miscellany, April, 1819, pp. 319–23. Review of *Autumnal Excursion.*

Port Folio (Philadelphia), July, 1819, pp. 41–46. Review of *Autumnal Excursion,* with copious extracts.

Quarterly Review, December, 1835, pp. 74–85. Review of *African Sketches,* ascribed to John Gibson Lockhart.

6. Obituary

Athenaeum, December 13, 1834, p. 908. This was reprinted in the *New Monthly Magazine,* XLIII (1835), pp. 137ff.

Index

Index

DATE DUE

GAYLORD			PRINTED IN U.S.A.